RETAIL
ANARCHY

RETAIL ANARCHY

SAM POCKER

A RADICAL SHOPPER'S ADVENTURES IN CONSUMPTION

Running Press
PHILADELPHIA · LONDON

9   8   7   6   5   4   3   2   1
Digit on the right indicates the number of this printing

Library of Congress Control Number: 2008944146

ISBN 978-0-7624-3439-8
Cover Illustration by Doug Fraser
Design by Joshua McDonnell
Edited by Jennifer Kasius
Typography: Eurostile, Mercury, and Machine

Running Press Book Publishers
2300 Chestnut Street
Philadelphia, PA 19103-4371

Visit us on the web!
www.runningpress.com

FOR JEAN & TALAS

With thanks to:

Jon Anderson
Amy Arutt
Amy Barker
H.T. Bear
Hank Bordowitz
Jackie Bullock
Ray & Carl Cooke
Bryna Darling
Rich & Karen Deiser
Steve DeMonke
Dave Derby
Chris Dicke
Alex Evenshteyn
Justin Field
Chris Frantz
Carl Freed
Brian Gettleman
Dawn & Mark Graham
Carrin Hare
Glen Harper
Kelly Marie Holmes
David Hood
Jennifer Johanos
Greg Jones
Jennifer Kasius
Bob Lang
Marbles LeGelebart
Barb Likos
Heidi MacDonald
DJ McDonald
Joshua McDonnell
Bud Miller

Debbie & Greg Miller
Jerome Moye
Kerry Nolan
Lynn O'Brien
James Olcott
Julie Parrish
Bobby Poirier
Doug Potash
Jerry Raynor
Sonya Riley
Jamie Roberts
Darlene & Bobby Roper
Winny Sagendorph
Glenn Schwartz
Margaret Shafer
Mark Shulman
Mary Jane Slaughter
Ellen Sluder
Tom Specht
Dede Stephens
Kristin Taylor
Maryanne Thompson
Jon Vena
John Voegtlin
Tina Weymouth
Everyone at Shidoobee, RC, RE,
TCC, HCW, CW, MA$, B$, FW,
SD, and SA
Mom & Dad
Sagendorphs, Bradys, Hoppers,
and Banachs everywhere.

Special thanks to Skip who sold me the Stones
ticket which ultimately inspired this book.

DISCLAIMER

This book is full of contradictions because it was written by a real person who, just like you, contradicts himself all the time.

This book is full of opinions; some are nice and some are not so nice, just like your own.

If you want to read a textbook about economics, you should go find one, but that's not my intent here. This book is a story about people and money, and it is intended only to make you think about how you spend your own. Call it a "Bedtime Story for Consumers."

Now get nice and comfortable, and remember, when you hear this sound **, turn the page.

TABLE OF CONTENTS

INTRODUCTION

"Hello Customer, Keep Erection Strong."

Walking into a Funkadelic concert, many patrons were witness to several men in various stages of intoxication and undress screaming and singing what seemed to be indecipherable noise for the better part of four hours.

Somewhere in his early thirties, George Clinton stood on a stage, tripping on LSD, dressed only in a bed sheet, and declared, "Free your mind and your ass will follow," and then proceeded to laugh uncontrollably for several minutes. It was, however accidentally, excellent advice for his audience.

True enough that George was mainly dealing with race relations, and not with consumer affairs, but the advice is easily adapted and equally as accidentally useful.

Before we can discuss George or how his work affects you, I need to explain a few things to you about the book you're about to read.

First of all, I am an economist, and therefore an expert about my topic. Fair enough? Let's examine my credentials. How did I come to be an economist? Did I attend a university and get a degree in business? No. Did I work for a financial firm? No. Have I ever taken a class in economics? No. As I discovered, all one needs to do in order to become an economist is simply to declare themselves to be one. All of Wall Street bases its decisions on the opinions of economists (admittedly, with legitimate credentials, I hope) but it is not actually necessary to do anything other than breathe in order to claim to be one. Having been an economist for almost five years, I have been offered multiple opportunities to speak to decision-makers at large corporations and their various industry conferences, and my thoughts have been taken under consideration when making business decisions that affect their various companies. Yet I have absolutely no formal training or experience of any kind. Pretty much all I have done is relay information that I have processed in the most primitive forms of common sense I could imagine, and then find my ideas receiving more and more attention. To George Clinton's detriment, I didn't even have to drop acid or wear a pair of tin-foil underpants in order to get people to listen to me.

Second, none of this happened by accident. For years, I would visit big box stores and watch customer service deteriorate and then come home and listen to economists on television place blame on abstract things like the price of oil to justify why retail sales were slipping. I've known for a long time that I had something I needed to say about the situation in retail but it's been only recently that I see how these things are affecting average consumers in such a profound way that it would be irresponsible for me not to speak out about them.

Third, I need to address a natural criticism of the work that follows. While any serious literary critic will rightfully note that this work is somewhat meandering (a "sprawling mess") and reads closer to a blog post than a proper book, it is entirely my intent for the work to have this aesthetic. This is due to the fact that the shopping centers which it criticizes have also been laid out in this very same fashion. While some first time authors may use another author's work as a blueprint, I used the floor plan of the King of

Prussia Mall in King of Prussia, Pennsylvania. Additionally, I have intentionally thrown out any fundamental literary structuring because this particular book was written for people who rarely read books. It is my sincere hope that after discovering and reading this one, they may begin to visit bookstores and libraries as opposed to the big box retailers who are presenting advertisements as faux-information, such as is found in commonplace "advertorials." If I have to hear my future mother-in-law regurgitate one more Fox News commentary as scientific fact, I'm going to take a baseball bat to her television.

Fourth, you may find yourself infuriated that I never fully introduce the characters or establishments. I take that as a raving compliment. In life, you may have discovered that you hear a great many stories about people you have never met or places you have never been. In writing this book to depict a slice of modern life which is being grossly ignored by the media, it is my hope to replicate a human experience and, as such, I present to you a conversation as is intended, not spoon-fed.

I trust that you, the reader, are of reasonable intelligence, and can figure out what is going on for yourself. If children can understand a Harry Potter book loaded with imaginary words, I'm quite confident that the average adult can comprehend a book about shopping.

Some people apparently get angry reading this work because of the information which is intentionally missing. For the more literary-minded among you, please understand that this is a device to elicit said emotion. When was the last time a book made you truly angry? So mad that you threw it across the room in disgust, then ran after it, picked it up, and kept reading? Those were the things I was looking at when writing it and, hopefully, you won't need to spackle and repaint small holes in your wall when you're done reading it. I have found it to be just wonderful to discover how many of my friends look at a film like *Triumph Of The Will* as a great work of art and speak of it with nothing but praise, yet are infuriated by my book about shopping.

Fifth, if all of this doesn't make you crazy (and strangely intrigued) already, this book is actually about dancing. Yes, celebratory physical expression of your emotions in public places are a key theme of the volume you hold in your hands. We all (hopefully) come to a point in our lives where we look around to discover that we are now the oldest people in the nightclub and feel a bit sad that we are too old to dance. I have discovered that with the proliferation of iPods (and the fact that in-store music is now interrupted frequently with advertisements for products) it has become socially acceptable to dance in public, and that with big box retailers dominating our landscape, the average department store is now bizarrely transformed into a discotheque of people dancing to their own individual playlists. This is why there are so many references to music in the book; because if you promise to read it cover to cover, I promise not only to make you throw it across the room in anger but to make you laugh, and want to dance. Go out and find yourself another economist who can offer you that. Dave Ramsey may want to hold your hand, but I'm here to burn your town down.

Sixth, many grocery stores hire mentally handicapped people to work as baggers, the people who are there to put your groceries in shopping bags while you pay for them. For many years this was a great idea because it gave the otherwise unemployable a job they could do, and provided a decent service to the customer.

When your bread was at the bottom of the bag under your carton of milk, you thought "oh well, they are doing a good service to the handicapped, and it's just a loaf of bread." It was excusable because they are handicapped, they can't help it, and we should all help out in the community.

This was, of course, all before bread became almost four dollars a loaf. I tend to look like some crazy antiques collector when I buy a loaf of bread now, making sure the date is as far out as possible and the loaf is near perfect for four dollars.

Having mentally handicapped baggers crush that loaf of bread is no longer excusable to me. While it is not the fault of the handicapped person, it is the fault of the store for continuing to employ them in this capacity. Please note I said in this capacity; I am not advocating that the handicapped be fired or penalized.

While I don't really want to see them lose their jobs and while I don't think a loaf of bread is worth $4, it is clear that in the situation the price of the item needs to come back down. However, we can't expect the manufacturer and retailer to do this. It's not fair to the handicapped guy to lose his job and no supermarket would be stupid enough to let these workers go for fear of a lawsuit. So who is the loser in this situation? The consumer, of course. This is a good part of my belief that retail is now at the forefront of anarchy, that for the first time in history the consumer has a real need to fight back. We are not talking about snake oil or false claims; we are talking about bread and milk. The consumer has been abused for too long, and is passively taking it, hence the fact that we are in a consumer-driven economy.

Imagine if every customer who bought a loaf of bread that was smashed up by the bagger brought it back to customer service and demanded that it be exchanged for an undamaged loaf; you would see real change as a result of the losses to either the store or manufacturer. At first the price would go up, which would then create competition by the other bakeries and ultimately drive the price back down once they realized the baggers were the bottleneck. While it may be tedious and unpleasant, making such demands is required of you as a responsible consumer.

While I am extremely sympathetic to mentally retarded employees, I am less than sympathetic to those perfectly intelligent employees who choose to act mentally retarded; in fact, to them I am downright aggressive and nasty.

Moments ago, I received an email solicitation with the subject line that read simply "Hello Customer! Keep Erection Strong!" Without opening the email, I already knew what the solicitation inside would offer. That is more than I can say for the hundreds of solicitations I receive every day with the names of obscure sales or the ubiquitous "Friends and Family" sale in which you always have to open the email just to find out how much of a percentage discount will be offered. It fascinates me that one person with no budget and a questionable command of the English language can advertise their penis enhancement product more effectively than a major corporation with a marketing budget.

It's the same thing that is wrong with the cashiers at one of my grocery stores. They are painfully lazy and couldn't care less about anything but their paycheck. Why are they so lazy? They're unionized, and the store is required to keep them employed unless they want to go through the intolerable process involved in negotiating with the union over letting one of them go. Now I have nothing at all against organized labor; I think the concept is completely on the right track and useful. However, when you have a really big union and a group of the employees decide to use it as an excuse not to work and the others don't say "hey, you're making us look bad," then organized labor may appear to both the employers and the customers to be a negative thing. In my case, everyone in that store decided to be lazy and none of the other union members seem to be telling them to shape up or ship out.

I absolutely hate this idiotic mentality retail employees have as if they are some sort of authority figure over you the customer. You can't blame them since the retailers all are starting to think this way now and encouraging it as part of the corporate culture, but that's okay. You can still fight back, you can still stick it to them, and you can still prove to them that no matter what they seem to think, they are a small piece of the overall retail puzzle, and that you have recourse— lots of it. You have more recourse than they have sense.

Now go to the register, pay for this book, use one of those frequent shopper coupons they email out every week (if you forgot it, that's okay, buy it anyway, because by the time you're done reading you will never forget one again), and bring it home so we can sit down and get to the "soup at hand." .

Thank You.

FIRST MOVEMENT
"WHAT ARE WORDS WORTH?"

GEORGE CLINTON WAS A HAIRDRESSER

True story. The man who began the most important American musical genre of the twentieth century was not a musician, but a hairdresser. Men hanging out at his barber shop in New Jersey wanted to form a Doo-Wop group known as The Parliaments and so off they went to change the world.

Before I tell you about funk music, I have to tell you about marketing. George Clinton may have been pumped full of drugs, but the man understood marketing better than the CEOs of many of today's Fortune 500 companies.

Initially, The Parliaments were signed to one record label, Revilot Records. After struggling for a few years with little success, Mr. Clinton discovered that the band could sign with another record label at the same time if they simply wrote and performed music under a different name. In 1968, Funkadelic, a band with the exact same members as The Parliaments, signed with Westbound Records. Having achieved some minor success by 1974, The Parliaments were no longer under contract to Revilot and went on to sign with Casablanca Records. This marketing method proved so successful that by the mid '80s the core members of what would be commonly referred to as "Parliament Funkadelic" would end up being the working members of over a dozen different band names spread out over a dozen or more record labels.

In 1979, Mr. Clinton even marketed this fact on the album cover for "Uncle Jam Wants You" (Funkadelic on Warner Brothers Records) featuring three props from his stage shows which were related to the titles of his hit songs. Imitating a famous pose from one of the Black Panthers, he is surrounded by the "Bop Gun" (Parliament on Casablanca Records), "Flashlight" (Parliament on Casablanca Records), and a flag from "One Nation Under A Groove" (Funkadelic on Warner Brothers Records).

Thus, he is symbolically expressing to the customer that no matter what the band name or record label, all of the music contained within is being written and performed by the same group of musicians. Never before and never since has anyone in the music industry so shrewdly pitted all of the record labels against each other in their never ending quest to sign the next big thing.

In creating a mythology, Clinton shrewdly realized that while the performers by name may begin to leave the group, if he created a stable of fictional characters which could be played by any musician that replaced them, he therefore could ensure the continuity of the work. By doing this he got so creative as to pit his own characters against each other. So the album "Uncle Jam Wants You" features notes on the cover art which outright insult the work of Parliament, as if to appear that the two groups were engaged in a feud when in fact, as I have stated, they were all comprised of the exact same people.

Ten years later, Prince would copy this routine (and in fact a good portion of the film *Purple Rain* is a takeoff on this idea) by creating faux groups such as The Time, Vanity 6, and The Family, all of which released albums composed and recorded almost entirely by Prince with only the lead vocal replaced and a different person or persons on the cover. Thus, in the film *Purple Rain*, a mythology was created when groups named "The Revolution" and "The Time" were fiercely competitive when in fact Prince was essentially a singer-songwriter using these groups as characters as a means of presenting his work.

What does any of this have to do with shopping or marketing?

Funk music operates on a simple premise. By emphasizing the first beat of every measure of the music as opposed to the second and fourth beats that soul music traditionally emphasizes, it allows the musicians to work as a group while individually expressing themselves; each could be playing an entirely different song simultaneously, but as long as the first beat of each measure they were playing was in time it would all sound perfect. It is generally regarded that James Brown invented this style of music, but as with anything in the history of music twenty people will claim to have done it first and none can ever supply proof.

All forms of dance music operate on the same principle that once you begin dancing your circulation will improve, providing a feeling of euphoria as dopamine is released into your system, and increased brain function as an additional result of your physical exercise. Set to music, it is practically like doing drugs (or Hostess Cupcakes).

Marketing operates on a simple premise as well —get the customer excited about the product or service by any means necessary, and once you have them on a roll, sell them the item while they are so happy they don't care what they are buying or how much they are spending.

Just look at the mythology and characters, with the soap-operaesque plotlines and drama that are now being used to sell everything from things like insurance (Geico Caveman) to shipping services (Dale Jarrett for UPS) to sandwiches (Jared for Subway) to computers (Dude You Got a Dell character). There are television commercials with sequels and, even worse, some brands actually have licensed merchandise like t-shirts and hats featuring the characters created solely for these television commercials.

As it turns out, a great many marketing gimmicks created by George Clinton in an attempt to screw the system have now been adopted by marketers in order to screw the customers. As customers, it is time to come up with some gimmicks of our own. Bop Guns, Flashlights, and "One Nation" flags flying high.

Thirty years later I would find myself in a Wal-Mart, bored, restless, hungry, tired, and cold. Recently out of the hospital, I was having trouble walking and somehow had decided that walking around the main perimeter of this store was a good form of exercise. I needed to put some music on my iPod that would get me moving; you know how everyone wants to listen to music with a good beat when they exercise. While I am not entirely sure why I decided to play "One Nation Under a Groove" on that day, it is clear to me now. Sometimes the most innocent and meaningless decisions can have the biggest impact on your life.

In this case, I found myself dancing alone in the aisles of a Wal-Mart, and suddenly it no longer looked like a Wal-Mart, it looked like a nightclub and I felt good. When I looked around at how miserable everyone was, filling shopping carts with things to make themselves happy, it occurred to me that it was a great waste of money. For it cost me nothing at all to have the time of my life just inches away from people who were spending hundreds of dollars and looked like they had just come from a funeral.

It further occurred to me that I was having more fun for free at a Wal-Mart than I had had at concerts where I had paid hundreds of dollars for a ticket and gone home completely disappointed. I swore to myself I was never going to pay that much money for a concert ticket again, and as I looked around at the cost of the things in the store I wondered what else I was never going to pay so much money for again.

Somewhere around the magazine rack I noticed the police coming into the store to confront someone at a checkout register. I turned down the music slowly, took out my headphones and was presented with my first dilemma.

WHY DO TERRORISTS
SHOP AT WAL-MART?

Every once in a while, a story will pop up on the news about terrorist cells buying up lots of prepaid cellphones at stores like Target and Wal-Mart. The stories are always the same: a van was pulled over, piled high with cellphones separated into bins of the phones, the batteries, and the packaging. Three or four men of "Middle Eastern descent" were in the vehicle and it had been driving from store to store clearing out all of the shelves, all of this paid for in cash. The articles or stories will always mention how a nuclear weapon could be detonated using a cellphone as a trigger.

When the shelves are restocked at those local stores, signs are put up noting that there is now a limit on the purchase of prepaid cellphones, and perhaps that you might have to show ID if you wish to purchase one.

Doesn't it seem kind of silly to you that terrorists would need that many cellphones to set off one bomb? Maybe there is more to the story? And why would the stores put up signs with limits if the terrorists had already been caught? How many terrorist cells are planning to blow up Manhattan with cellphones and nuclear weapons exactly? And if you were planning to do so, why go all the way to Wal-Mart to get the phones? Wouldn't it be easier to buy them in bulk on eBay or something?

Prepaid cellphones are a classic promotion gone wrong. The wholesale on these phones is usually in the range of $100. A cellphone service provider will buy them in bulk, program them to work on their network, and then package them up with their logo and information, only to sell them at places like Wal-Mart for a mere thirty dollars. So why take a loss? Because they are hoping to hook the customer into spending thousands of dollars in service over the lifetime of the phone. By attracting people with bad credit who couldn't be approved for contract service, they are able to sell each minute at a premium price, for a thousand minutes may cost $75 to a customer on a contract, but on a prepaid basis, those same thousand minutes can be resold for $250 to a customer with bad credit, desperate for the use of a cellphone.

This leads us to the "terrorists," independent cellphone resellers who realize they can pay $30 cash for a phone that is worth $100, and resell it on eBay for $50. I ask you, what could possibly be more American than that?

Because they are independent and do not have the resources of either the cellphone service providers or the big box retailers they are taking advantage of and competing against, instead of being portrayed as inventive and aggressive entrepreneurs, they are portrayed as "terrorists."

As of this writing, police still have no leads on countless violent crimes, but they do have the time and resources to harass entrepreneurs who are attempting to make a buck in a legal and ethical way (and at the expense of companies who are trying to exploit the impoverished, no less). Why? Because someone at the cellphone service provider said it was clearly a crime to take advantage of their bad promotion and the retailer (in the interest of continuing to do business as usual) as an accomplice concurred with the claim.

On many occasions, I have had the opportunity to purchase large numbers of cellphones at a substantial discount using all sorts of rebates and coupons and on occasion I have had a store manager refuse to sell them to me in any quantity. When I contact the corporate headquarters of these chain stores and ask them what the problem is, they instruct the store manager to sell me the phones, after which he usually claims that the police had asked him not to because "drug dealers use them."

No matter who you are or where you shop, there is always some fabricated reason why the store does not want you to buy prepaid cellphones in bulk, but the real reason is always the same: because they are a loss leader item that is constantly sold far below their fair market value. If the stores sell too many phones to one person in a reasonably short amount of time, they are often harassed by the cellphone providers who as a "courtesy" inform the police that "drug dealers" or "terrorists" may be trying to buy up all of the phones Since the people with the financial risk in these sales cannot control the secondary market, they attempt to control the primary market.

You will never hear that on the news; you will only hear about how terrorists cannot get their hands on every cellphone in sight quickly enough.

FREE PEPSI

I just threw out 48 cans of Pepsi. Last February, CVS offered a $10 rebate when you bought four 12-packs of the stuff and then I used coupons on top of that. I made around $10 buying 48 cans, between the coupons, rebate, credit card points, and the CVS Extra Care Bucks. If you don't understand what all of that means, don't worry, we'll get into it later. Just understand that I made $10 buying it.

The problem here is I don't really drink a lot of soda and I had no idea soda expired. I figured I was buying a year's supply, since I roughly drink one can a week. Sure enough, soda actually expires, and it really does taste awful after a while. So there I was, up to my ass in soda cans, pouring it all down the drain. All of the natural resources wasted on making it, packaging it, shipping it, and then paying me to take it. Now they will waste more natural resources treating the water and recycling the cans.

Already you're thinking, "that is so wasteful; he should have drunk the Pepsi before it went bad." That stuff is like poison to me. One can a week is really more than I could, or probably even should, drink. Regardless, I got paid to take it. It took me no more than 20 minutes to buy it, bring it home, and ultimately throw it out, and for this I made $10. The current federal minimum wage is $5.15 an hour, which I just beat by 400%.

For their parts in this waste, both CVS and Pepsi can record the "sale" of this soda, even though both contributed to paying my cut, Pepsi via the manufacturer's coupons and CVS via the Extra Care Bucks. Since both record it as a "sale," they both can claim to have record sales, and as a result see an improvement in their stock price.

This is a basic example of the world I live in where manufacturers and retailers pay me to take their lousy merchandise off their hands. Meanwhile, down the street at my local grocery store, I watch in horror as people who make minimum wage pay the full retail price for the same cans of Pepsi.

I'm going to sound like my mother here for a minute, but these people shouldn't be drinking all that soda. Not to mention that on paper they simply can't afford it.

It is not lost on me that while some outrageous percentage of the world has no access to clean drinking water I am standing in my kitchen being paid to dispose of intentionally altered drinking water with the end purpose of increasing the value of a stock and ultimately the profit of a shareholder.

Lest anyone think I am against Pepsi or Coke, every soda company, and for that matter just about every major food manufacturer, runs similar promotions which result in a similar outcome (i.e., I get paid to dispose of their products) these days. This is not any kind of political or activist agenda. I just feel that people are not seeing this take place the way I am seeing it take place and I want to help you see the absurdity of it.

We all know someone who likes either one food or beverage SO much that they have taken to buying it by the case at a warehouse club. We always think of them as a funny character, but it's alarming when you step back and look at how many funny characters there are.

WHY DO I HAVE TO TELL MY BANK THAT I AM GOING ON VACATION?

It is a positively absurd question, but one which needs to be asked. After returning home from Florida recently, I discovered a half dozen messages on my voicemail from my bank inquiring as to my whereabouts. When I returned the call, I discovered an option which would let me inform them that I was going to travel in the future, so that they would know there was no fraud being committed with my debit card. If the replacement of checks and even cash is ideally to make spending money more convenient, is this not thoroughly negated by the need to call my bank and tell them I am going on vacation? And if the information was stolen, which would ultimately be more valuable to a criminal? A list of debit card numbers, or a massive list of names and addresses of people who wouldn't be home at a given time? It is an incredibly stupid system, with a massive flaw, but the spin doctors in marketing have come up with the phrase "for your protection," which sounds ominously like a contraceptive device. Contraceptives, however, suffer from the same flaw: you have to be smart enough to use them. And so there is a massive population of stupid people, many of whom have now been trained to call the bank and tell them about their travel plans. Thank God we live in a free country where we do not need permission from our government to travel freely— we only need permission from our banks.

WAL-MART IS A VERY EXPENSIVE STORE

Why are people so trusting? At the Apple store, when they hire some teenage kid and slap a t-shirt on him that says "Genius" do people actually think he is? Do you become a genius just because your t-shirt says you are? No, of course not. So why then, when a big store moves into town, with the clear intent to put every other store in your town out of business and states in big letters on the facade of the building that they have the lowest prices, do you trust them?

There are two formats for selling packaged goods (which includes groceries) and they are essential to understanding retail:

Hi-Lo

High Price & Low Price - This is the traditional format you're used to in which most items are sold at their full retail price and occasionally go on sale for a substantially discounted price.

EDLP

Every Day Low Price – The format that Wal-Mart pioneered and many other stores have begun to copy. In this format, nothing ever goes on sale, but is sold at a price somewhere in the middle of the "Hi-Low" continuum mentioned above.

So if you were to shop at your normal everyday supermarket which utilized a Hi-Lo format, an item on sale would be considerably cheaper than the same item at a Wal-Mart Supercenter. Should you be smart enough to use a coupon on that item while it was on sale, Wal-Mart would suddenly appear to be a very expensive store and that's the truth that has eluded a great deal of the American public. Wal-Mart IS a very expensive store, which has created two cultural faux pas that irritate me. The first is the news reporter, business analyst, or any other non-fiction presenter who refers to Wal-Mart as a "discounter," "discount store," or anything similar. The second, as I've previously alluded to, is that customers are so stupid in believing this nonsense that many grocery and other retail chains have decided to play along and emulate the formula.

When this happens, it's a goldmine for coupon shoppers because every other store in the area works with the manufacturers to offer tremendous sales on staple items and the manufacturers go to town putting out high value coupons for their products in that market. Who loses? All those dumb customers who never bothered to ask what "Every Day Low Price" actually means and those who believe what some letters glued to a Wal-Mart storefront tell them to believe. Oh, and all of those business analysts who I will never trust again.

Let me tell you about my last trip to Wal-Mart, a story you will never hear a financial analyst repeat. The woman in front of me was buying three enormous bags of dog treats, eight multipacks of Trident chewing gum, and a negligee. Halfway through paying, she farted and the cashier covered her face with her uniform. After the woman had paid and walked away, the cashier told us we had to wait a moment as she went and got a deodorizer spray and proceeded to spray it all over the register, all over us, our merchandise, and the surrounding area. Another cashier stopped ringing up a customer and walked over, "Oh no, I had a man in here the other day doing all that; I told him it's too hot today, Mister, you can't do that in here."

I looked over to a third register where the cashier had a different excuse for each customer who wanted to pay for something. "Ten items or less," "cash only," "credit only." Jean turned to me and said, "people wearing blue shirts only," and we burst out laughing.

Finally, the cashier went back to work and rang us up, but continued talking about how badly the customer before us had farted.

There we stood in the largest chain store in the world at one of the highest generating locations of the company and the whole enterprise had been brought to a standstill by flatulence.

COSTCO

Men and women shop differently. There is this male need to *go shopping once and never again*, to overbuy everything as if it were an act of defiance against the oppressive female regime that couldn't keep up with the pace of pretzel consumption at home.

The men then stand in line at the warehouse club impatiently, since they've already had two cups of Starbucks and a Pepsi at 10 a.m.

Their overfilled cart drops merchandise on the floor and instead of simply picking it up and putting it back on top of the pile of crap in their carts they slowly begin the daredevil relay race of trying to walk back to where they found the item and exchange it for a "fresh" one.

Halfway into this quest, they simply abandon the item they had dropped on top of a store display of sweaters, pants, or frozen lobster tails.

From there, they then attempt to make it through the checkout again without anything else falling or breaking. Sometimes they ask the person behind them to watch their cart while they run to the snack bar for another soda and maybe a hot dog —and while they're at it perhaps some chips, oh and some cookies, and maybe another hot dog. The whole time they are barking away on Bluetooth headsets.

By the time they are at the register they have to pee so badly they take out their self-imposed frustration on the cashiers. For their part, the cashiers passive-aggressively fight back at the customer by "forgetting" to tell them to hold onto their receipts so that illiterate "security guard" (read: old man who lost his glasses and is wearing a windbreaker and a baseball cap with the logo from either another retailer, a bank, or a security firm printed on it) at the door may observe the receipt's existence and acknowledge it with a line, a punched hole, or the meaningless signing of his/her initials. It's sort of a formal custom which also involves him making a bit of a circle with his head, as if to say he sees everything in your cart, and yes, it does match the merchandise on the receipt. Not that I am encouraging anyone to shoplift, but it's probably the only store in the world where you could practically sneak out with an entire sofa under your coat and no one would say a word. If Dr. Seuss had invented a store, I bet it would have been a warehouse club.

Once they've completed packing up the car, the men forget that they had to pee, and angrily get back on the road. Halfway home they realize they have to pee again and drive like maniacs, shouting at everyone. Finally draining their bladders, they hit the fridge for another cold soda before going to unpack the car, whereupon they discover anything frozen has now melted (in bulk).

TARGET

Some of you are sitting there thinking, "I never shop like that. I don't know anyone who shops like that. We are civilized grown-ups. We wear sweaters, Keds, and we are paying members of our local PBS station."

That's true, you don't shop like that; your shopping habits are even worse.

Target shoppers are all the same. You buy one 12-pack of soda at a time. If you don't believe me, try this yourself. Go to Target and watch people check out. Almost every single customer buys a 12-pack of soda.

Trying to read a Target advertisement makes you look as if you're partaking in some form of performance art. Whoever writes the copy was heavily inspired by David Byrne's work in "Your Action World." Talk about art imitating life imitating art. Completely meaningless phrases are written by the marketing department which are intended to feign enthusiasm on the part of the sales staff, yet poorly convey any information or inspire true enthusiasm from the consumer. The meat and potatoes of the Target circular "Dollar Week."

What is "Dollar Week"?

Does it mean everything is on sale for a dollar? Does it mean everything is a dollar off? It never seems to mean either of these things. I have certainly seen "Dollar Week" advertised more than six times in a year, so clearly it's not an annual holiday, like President's Day, for example. I've routinely sent letters to Target asking what "Dollar Week" means and I've never gotten a written response. When you call to ask each operator has a different story, so there is no official corporate answer to that question.

"Our lowest prices ever!"

It's like calling KISS "The HOTTEST band in the world!" What scientific instrument does one use to gauge a band's "Hotness"? The phrase itself is silly. "Our lowest prices ever!" On which item or items? And wouldn't inflation technically make this claim impossible? Sure, you could say that many of the items didn't exist before a certain timeframe, and therefore inflation wouldn't apply, but we are speaking in such vague terms. Are we talking about entire product categories?

Target was founded in 1962, so can we automatically rule out things like bars of soap, pants, and chewing gum? Well, of course we can, and while it's bizarre enough to consider how many items at Target didn't even exist in 1962, you're left with quite a number of unanswered questions from these four words, "Our lowest prices ever."

By the time you're done thinking about it, you couldn't care less about what they sell or how much it is because you're now in dire need of a nap and perhaps a sandwich. Oh and maybe some soup, hmm pickles would be good too. But I'm too tired now to think about making a sandwich. I'm still overwhelmed from the blaring four words printed in the Target ad.

You can just picture David Byrne sitting around the house getting stoned, sticking a Polaroid camera down his pants and calling the result, "Our lowest price ever!" The man is a genius, what can you say?

Better still, look for the people buying organizers of any kind; they always have twice as much merchandise in their cart than will fit in the organizer they are buying to clean up a mess they already have at home. It never fails.

What's wrong with buying one 12–pack of soda at a time? You're paying for it and you're paying full price for it. I just poured a whole bunch of the shit down the drain and here you're spending perfectly good money on it. What are you thinking? Target is just Wal-Mart with less selection and higher prices. Yes, it's true that they have limited edition products made by designers, that they are more "socially conscious," and that the stores are much cleaner than Wal-Mart —but for how long?

I think Target is a great example of a store where the employees are neither cunning nor active salespeople; in my opinion the ones I've met are simply lazy and stupid. I have flipped out on more than a few Target "team members." What team are they on? The Special Olympics bobsledding team, if you ask me.

Target is a great act of deception; the store is exceptionally clean and well-designed. The exclusive merchandise is extremely pleasing to the eye and the demographic who shops there is mostly female. On the surface, Target seems to be a nearly perfect retail store.

One day when I was in a Target I saw a video game that had been on 90% clearance from the previous season. When it rang up at the register, no price would come up, since 90% off of the last price was less than a penny. A store manager had to be called. It turned out that no matter what I was willing to pay, the item couldn't be sold to me as it was technically "discontinued."

The manager said, "I would really love to sell this to you but I have no way to do so." Being my usual inquisitive self, I asked him what he would do with the video game and he told me that it would be sent back to the "main warehouse" and sold as a closeout that would then end up at "a flea market."

Now I knew perfectly well this was not what was going to happen; either it would be shipped back to the manufacturer for credit, or end up being destroyed and thrown in a dumpster, but I didn't argue. Either he was too ignorant or he was lying, and since he wouldn't sell it to me anyway there was no point in dragging out the conversation.

To you I will say this: no matter what they did with the item it would require more natural resources be wasted on it. Target could just as easily put a price on it and sell it to me, but they refused; they simply demanded to waste more natural resources on it for no reason other than they couldn't figure out how to handle the accounting of the item any other way. It is this kind of pig-headedness at the top that trickles down through the entire company and ends up, as I said, with a bunch of perfectly healthy and intelligent people acting mentally retarded because it is just easier for them to do so. If no customer ever learns how to dispute them properly, it will continue indefinitely at the expense of the consumers' money, time, and our environment, which will further cost the consumer more time and money.

Those of you who are "power shoppers" already know the third possibility of where the video game would end up and that would of course be a Goodwill thrift store. You know this because you see all the other Target store-brand items that end up there. But of course the term "thrift store" is about as misleading as you can get.

Almost all of the Target custom-manufactured items have their original retail price printed on the packaging, which Target charges for a season and then marks down. Goodwill "thrift stores" almost always sell the same items ABOVE the cost marked on the package, for no good reason other than greed.

The item was donated to them with the understanding they would sell it at a bargain price to consumers as an incentive to shop at the "thrift store"; in exchange Goodwill keeps the consumers' money to use towards its charitable causes. While we should all donate money to charity and support causes like Goodwill and others, why must we be so rudely charged a high price for it? The fact that a charity would overcharge for merchandise in something called a "thrift store" is an embarrassment and anyone dumb enough to think it was a great deal is even more of an embarrassment.

Yes, I understand not *every* Goodwill thrift store overcharges for Target private-label merchandise (but pretty much every one I have ever visited does), and *no*, I do not think you should *stop* shopping there if you already do, but I *do* think they should be more upfront about what the store is: a second-hand store that exists to earn donations for a charity, not a "Thrift Shop" which implies that there is a discounted value to the merchandise being sold.

To add insult to injury, several Target stores around me have stopped clearance of seasonal merchandise early in order to make more money displaying full priced merchandise on the shelf for next season. This is further proof to the educated consumer that Target is not truly a discount retailer and is not interested in making sure their customers get the first opportunity to purchase the discontinued merchandise at an appropriate price. And to that extent, Target is a deception. I am not suggesting Wal-Mart or Kmart are any better, but you have never seen either of those chains invest so much time and money to try to act "above" each other in an aesthetic sense the way Target does.

Nor is Target free of the idiocy plague that sweeps just about every other big box retailer, in which the corporate headquarters are endlessly involved in a game of "operator" regarding their various store policies. This is a problem which involves two stores that do not follow the same ground rules because the two store managers cannot pay attention long enough or communicate well enough to their employees the requests of the corporate headquarters.

We have had many situations in which two Target stores a few miles from each other will have polar opposites for coupon policies, meaning one will accept a manufacturers' coupon for a certain item and the other one will not. I personally have taken to carrying around a letter from the corporate headquarters which details the company's coupon policy, so if I end up in an argument with an egotistical and power hungry store manager (and I usually do), I can simply show him the letter when he tells me I don't know what I am talking about.

Forget my bitching and moaning for a minute; let's step back and look at retail anarchy here. You see, every Target store has a kiosk for you to access bridal registries, examine your Target charge card bill, or visit target.com. Each of these kiosks has a printer attached to it for the purpose of printing out the bridal registries. When you visit target.com one of the options is to print out in-store coupons. Sure, you could waste your own ink and paper printing them out at home, but why bother when Target essentially gives you the gun to shoot itself in the foot with? A great example was a coupon for $1 off any cereal by a particular manufacturer. Target sold single serving cups of the cereal for 79 cents.

All you had to do was go into a Target store, print out a hundred copies of the coupon for free at the kiosk, clean off the shelves of cereal, and bring it to the register. When the cashier flipped out on you, all you had to do was pull out the letter from Target corporate showing that the store's coupon policy fully allowed this transaction to take place, and you could fill your car with breakfast cereal from here to eternity, free of charge.

Do you think I didn't make a face at anyone I saw actually buying the stuff for the next six months?

For most people, this would be a once-in-a-lifetime experience. Something to tell their grandchildren about, the crazy day they filled the car with a stack of breakfast cereal so tall that they couldn't see out of the windows. For me, it's just another day in the life of a retail anarchist.

BET YOUR BOTTOM DOLLAR

Let's play a quick game. Go get an index card and a pen. Or if life is short and cheap for you, just write in the margin and rip out this page.

Anyway, here's our game. We are each going to invent a packaged food product that there is no way either of us would eat, even if we were paid to consume it. I'll get you started. Here's mine, "StrepCakes" —StrepCakes are the tasty snack-cakes prepared exclusively by people with bacterial infections and no plastic gloves or hairnets.

Okay, now you go.

Not bad, but here's the game, I want you to fold up the index card and put it in your wallet. Then wait about five years. I can nearly guarantee that you will see the item as an actual packaged food for sale in a "dollar store." Many of you may have already seen "StrepCakes" already for sale in "dollar stores," but under the generic, not the brand name.

Common sense should suggest not ingesting anything found in a "dollar store," but many of us think with our stomachs. The real crime is people who now buy meat and produce at the "upscale" dollar stores. Two of the largest chains, "Dollar General" and "Family Dollar," both look like medical clinics to me, and I should know, I've spent plenty of time in medical clinics. The third competitor, "Dollar Tree," is a world unto itself. The last time I was in Dollar Tree I watched people shop for junk while the radio played a Carrie Underwood song in which she begged Jesus to "take the wheel." If Jesus Christ really was her savior, he should have taken her checkbook and credit cards first.

The dollar store concept started with the same premise as Wal-Mart: to sell some items very cheaply and to sell the rest at an inflated price masked by the tremendous value of the few cheap items. It's just a small psychological trick, which is why people fill their shopping carts at the dollar store with things they will never use— because "it's only a dollar!"

Novelty is another key. When dollar stores first started springing up everywhere people would practically clean them out just because everything was "so cheap," and certainly most people understood the trick when they saw a 25-cent pack of gum being sold for a dollar, but they just ignored it. As the trend became more stable, gradually more and more products were overpriced, like plastic spray bottles, composition books, kitchen sponges, the sort of items that should just cost 25 or 50 cents.

FOR THOSE WITH NO COMMON SENSE, WE SALUTE YOU!

An important misconception I wish to dispel up front is that the food sold in dollar stores is closeout or overstock. While some of the dry goods are, a majority of the food is manufactured and sold directly for and to dollar stores.

Some people still wonder what is wrong with consuming edibles purchased from a dollar store and I suppose it's a reasonable question. What exactly is the difference between a microwaved cheeseburger from the Dollar Tree compared to a 99-cent double cheeseburger from McDonald's? A penny and an extra burger?

Let's start with the presumption that the contents of the burger are beef. People assume that if a package says "100% All-Beef Patty" that the hamburger is made entirely of beef. There are two issues here; the first is that when someone is trying to sell something of value for an extremely low price, they are usually lying.

We all know it's a lie when someone offering us a used car too cheaply says, "it was only driven by a little old lady to the store twice a week." That roughly translates to "the odometer has been rolled back, and only after an extensive amount of body work."

Why then do we trust "100% All-Beef Patty"? Who has more to lose? The guy selling a $5,000 car or the guy selling a $1 hamburger? If the car salesman will so blatantly misrepresent, why then won't the hamburger salesman?

I have encountered the "100% All-Beef Patty" in a dollar store and read all of the other ingredients in the patty on the back of the package. They don't lie *per se*; rather, it is simply an issue of semantics. All of the meat in the patty is in fact beef. It's that the beef is padded with lots of non-meat items and it is the non-meat items that are always the issue.

What's the difference between buying this $1 hamburger at a dollar store as opposed to a supermarket? Supermarkets are regulated, often requiring various licenses and subject to routine health inspections. Supermarket employees are often required by the various states in which they are located to be trained in food safety and proper handling techniques. Not so for many dollar stores; they often only stock the items which skirt the laws for requiring expensive licenses and thus pallets of frozen food may sit out at room temperature for hours before being placed in the freezers. Same thing goes for rodent control regarding the packaged foods on the shelves.

One of my most horrifying finds was the twin chili dog manufactured by a company ominously named "The Pride of Iowa." Indeed, if this product is truly the pride of Iowa, I shudder to think at what the shame of Iowa might be.

In the box of two chili dogs for a dollar sits a plastic tray, two hot dogs made of beef, pork, chicken and turkey parts (commonly referred to as "Lips & Assholes") nestled in a bun that smells like moldy socks topped with what can only be described as a bean-based diaper explosion messily splattered all over it, so much so that more of the "chili" resides on the sides of the bun than on top.

Outside the box, a sticker holds the flap sealed, the package reads "TRY ME" as if Lewis Carroll had placed it there himself, just to see if anyone actually would. The slogan "Crossroads of Quality and Value" is printed on the side of the box, presumably to inform the consumer at which intersection the animals contained within were scraped off of the road.

While I won't bore you with a play-by-play accounting of the ingredients or the various misspellings on the box, I should tell you that at one point I read the word "Dog" and screamed a few expletives aloud, only to realize moments later that it was the subject heading for the hot dog's ingredient list.

The lack of information, such as the true name of the manufacturer, on the packaging should be alarming, such as the box I found that displayed the country of origin as simply "Produced by Europe." The band? I wondered.

My favorite private label brand was the "Liberty Gold" canned pineapples with a picture of the Statue of Liberty on the can. This was a tragic mistake in branding on two levels: the first is that New York City is not exactly known for its pineapple production, and the other is that the product was manufactured in Indonesia.

There are other issues with the trade dress, such as the licensing of medical associations logos to make the product appear healthy. The American Heart Association, for example, will license (for a fee, of course) their insignia to food manufacturers selling products low in sodium or saturated fat, two of the main triggers for heart disease. This seems to make sense until you realize that some of the foods they have licensed look so dangerous that they might as well have cyanide in them, so long as there is no salt or saturated fat.

Although the twin chili dogs had me thinking I should have picked up an antibiotic on my way home, they were nothing compared to the baked clams. The city of Gloucester, Massachusetts is known for a great many things, such as its casino cruises, its Dunkin Donuts' parking lot in which a majority of the town's residents seem to spend their summer holding a 24-four hour tailgate party from June to August, and its nautical-themed seafood restaurants that turn into after-hours nightclubs. More recently it even made the news for a pact between 17 teenage girls who all tried to intentionally get pregnant before the end of the school year.

With such grand accomplishments, it can now add that it is home to a company that provides dollar store chains with baked clams in the most unsecured food packaging I have ever seen in my life. Packaged food should not be sold on a Styrofoam tray simply wrapped in cellophane, as it could easily be opened and resealed, or opened, defecated on by rodents, discovered the following morning, resealed, and put back on a retail shelf. Certainly based on its colorful history, it seems Gloucester is not necessarily the American city in which we should be entrusting our food safety.

While you might correctly note that Gloucester is a fishing community, there is a considerable difference between selling raw fish and packaged prepared food, especially clams.

NO MYTH

China gets blamed for so many things, some of them true and some of them false. Of course, there are issues with China, such as the fact that the FDA admits they catch less than two percent of the Chinese imports coming into the United States which are unfit for human consumption. One of the more interesting things that the FDA stops from coming in are foods treated with Nitrofuran, which, in layman's terms, appears to be a veterinary drug used on fish to kill bacteria. Besides the fact that Nitrofuran causes cancer and is described as being used to "control disease," which I might add in broken English, "control" does not necessarily mean "prevent," why is there bacteria in the fish? Because China dumps anything they can find into any body of water they can find, that's why. Why do they do that? Because there is rampant overpopulation, which makes human waste literally unmanageable. They might as well call it 繁體中文版 (translation: "Final Solution Fish Company").

That is not to say we don't produce inedible crap here in the United States as well, a box of three ribeye steaks for $5 that claims to be treated with bromelain (an "enhancer") and ficin (to kill parasites). What really bothers me is not the fact that the company who manufactured these steaks brags on their website that they are a top provider of meat to airlines (yes, you read that correctly), but that the USDA reports that they are constantly catching Chinese companies trying to smuggle meat into the United States, labeling the shipments with false contents such as "Dried Lily Flower."

Let's face it: if you're selling microwaveable sandwiches for $1, you want to use the cheapest materials you can find. It is inconceivable that one or two manufacturers of the deceptively named "convenience foods" category of products are unscrupulous enough to use this stuff if they can get their hands on it and our government is admitting that they are probably getting their hands on it.

The problems with this meat, especially the poultry, is that it does not go through any of the same regulatory inspection processes that our meats do. In China, everything must be done as cheaply as possible; thus the chickens are often fed pig shit (literally), perhaps from pigs that may have been infected with influenza. This means that a mutated flu which humans are not resistant to, the avian flu, is a health nightmare just waiting to happen.

Why doesn't the Chinese government address the issue? Because they have so many people that they can't possibly kill them off fast enough. This is a country that suffers from such overpopulation that the government mandates abortions on any family that already has more than one child. With these kinds of problems, is it any mystery why the Chinese government couldn't care less if the "food" gets exported to the United States and kills off as many of us as quickly as possible? Why train an army or buy weapons when you can ship off toxic poultry in a box marked "Dried Lily Flower" and get your enemy to thank you for selling it to them?

The most famous problem thus far was the tainted pet food, discovered in April of 2007, which raised the issue of wheat gluten. Up to this point, most of us had never really heard of or thought much about wheat gluten. I had some questions, as I'm sure you did as well.

What is wheat gluten?

It is a pulp composed of wheat flour without starch; it's kind of like eating papier maché.

What was it doing in pet food?

It was used, as it is in human food, to bulk it up. As it is flavorless and has the same texture as meat but is a heck of a lot cheaper, you can mash it up with any kind of meat and make it appear as if you had twice as much meat as you actually had. Most of your dollar store sandwiches contain wheat gluten or a similar faux-meat (look for "modified food starch" on the label) blended with real meat.

Why was it dangerous?

This particular batch of wheat gluten had been mixed with melamine.

What is melamine?

It is basically a form of plastic; while considered minimally toxic, it could lead to reproductive damage, bladder or kidney disease. Reproductive damage can lead to more dollar store customers.

Why was the wheat gluten mixed with melamine?

To thicken it, as melamine is cheaper than wheat gluten. In order to cut costs, the Xuzhou Anying Biologic Technology company basically mixed a thickener in a thickener.

Those damn Chinese Commie bastards really are trying to kill us! I'm only going to eat organic American-made food from now on!

While it is true that the Chinese government denied any problem and wouldn't allow FDA inspectors into the country to investigate the problem for over three weeks, this statistic seems to be a somewhat political distraction. At the same time we began prohibiting imports of Chinese-made wheat gluten, the FDA kindly asked two feed companies in the United States to pretty-please stop using melamine in their fish and shrimp feed. Had you purchased fish which had eaten this very same feed, it technically could have been USDA certified organic.

All of this is something of a moot point. I've said that the FDA admits that it catches far less than two percent of the illegal imports coming into our country. So there may the basis for the ancient Chinese proverb "Eat Shit and Die."

There have been many dollar-store-item recalls in record numbers, such as hot-glue guns (470,000 manufactured) and magnetic dart boards (870,000 manufactured), which have added some much-needed bulk to our landfills, but to this day there is only one recall of a food item at a dollar store: Pokemon branded Valentine's Day candy. Metal fragments were found inside the package.

While I understand that all press releases have a touch of advertising in them, with the intent of generating business by presenting a story that may be considered news, there are limits to bad taste. I don't know, maybe it's just me, but if I had been the sole retailer of potentially deadly children's candy, I might have had just a touch more tact than to end my press release about the recall with a full paragraph boasting about how great my chain of stores is.

"We are so sorry we killed your three-year-old son, but please do stop by the next time you need cheap batteries!"

Dollar General did it shamelessly and not one person called them on it. Luckily, as far as I can tell, not one person was injured or killed by the product, but at the time the press release was issued the company had no idea if anyone had been hurt by it yet. It's scummy, plain and simple—there is no other word to accurately describe it. Who would issue such a press release? A scumbag, that's who.

It's not like anyone who might have been affected by this might have made much noise about it anyway, as in the course of writing this book I have stumbled upon a dumbfounding statistic.

Better Business Bureau Complaints Over a Three-Year Period		
STORE	**# OF LOCATIONS**	**# OF COMPLAINTS**
DOLLAR TREE	3411	1
DOLLAR GENERAL	8000	12
FAMILY DOLLAR	6430	8
KMART	1388	14,131

Please keep in mind that these numbers are *not* exact, as some stores opened and closed during that period, and I only counted the complaints made against the corporate headquarters of each company, not the individual locations. It has been my experience that the numbers of complaints that are made against the headquarters usually offer a more accurate reflection of the overall situation. You're free to disagree, but the numbers speak for themselves.

There is one additional factor here: the Kmart stores are much larger than the dollar stores, but in doing very rough math I estimated that Kmart received one complaint for every 11.8 million feet of floor space, as opposed to the other three *combined*, which received only one complaint for every 5.7 million feet of floor space.

I'm sure the same cocksucker who wrote that Dollar General press release would tell you that the discrepancy is due to the fact that customers truly preferred Dollar General to Kmart, but I beg to differ. It is my personal opinion, based on many hours spent watching consumers at all four chains, that the discrepancy is due to the fact that the target demographic for these dollar chains is either functionally illiterate or recently immigrated and thus unaware that an organization such as the Better Business Bureau even exists. Additionally, customers are more likely to throw something in the garbage and say it's not worth the hassle than to complain about a $1 item which is more expensive when purchased at Kmart.

The fact of the matter is that they could hang up a giant sign in a dollar store that reads "POOR PEOPLE SMELL" and nobody would complain. Nobody seems to be complaining about the packaged lunch meat with high fructose corn syrup in it. How else do you explain a person purchasing a $1 box of sandwich bags manufactured with a mere quantity of eight inside? A display of $1 brown paper "grab bags" has been ravaged, ripped open by customers who didn't understand what was contained in them. In another aisle, a display box reads "Educational Posters," and holds shrink-wrapped posters of Spiderman, Jimmie Johnson, and Dale Earnhardt Jr.

On my last trip there, I found one (and only one) bumper sticker for sale, and it read simply "Loser." I don't know what is worse, the level of low self-esteem one must have to shop at this store, or the fact that the store seems to understand that about their customers and gleefully exploit it.

In 2006, Dollar General announced it would be closing 400 stores and opening 300 new ones. Think about that for a second. Closing *four hundred* stores is a major undertaking, but then why would you go and open 300 more? You know when you're looking for a job and you send out tons of resumes hoping that one of them gets you the job? It's kind of like that. They open the stores and hope that the people in the surrounding area are stupid enough to shop there. If the consumers turn out to be too smart to shop there, they simply close the doors and move somewhere else. This is not what a retailer selling a quality product at a fair price should ever have to do. While I'm sure the annual report claims they move for more favorable real estate terms, why the hell would they have opened a store with poor real estate terms in the first place (and have made the same mistake 399 more times)? In 2009 they plan to close 450 stores and open 700 new ones. What is all of that musical chairs doing to the environment? Who ever heard of a business plan like this? I'm sure some of you are thinking about all of the jobs people lose when they move, but the balance sheet shows that they lose almost nothing in paying off the employees compared to the merchandise they take a loss on to sell at store closing clearance sales. This whole crazy enterprise still earns money, with the Dollar General CEO earning a total of $2.5 million in 2007. I am an economist, not a financial analyst (as I have not yet completed reading my "For Dummies" book on the subject), but I wonder if it's not all some sort of elaborate accounting game.

I personally believe that these stores' actions are reprehensible: they are targeting the uneducated in selling these discount foods of poor nutritional quality, made with questionable (and I think I have been very clear what is so questionable about them) contents, and at prices which pound-for-pound are actually rather expensive.

When customers talk of value, there is none. You can do better at a supermarket on a salad dressing sale than you ever will at a dollar store. The salad dressing routine goes like this: salad dressing goes on sale all the time for $1 a bottle (usually advertised as "10 for $10," but you only need to buy one). Then you have a coupon for 50 cents off salad dressing that will double at a store that does double coupons. So now you have free salad dressing.

A second coupon will say, "Purchase a salad dressing and get $1 off lettuce," which you can usually find a sale on bags of salad for $1. Now you have free salad dressing and free lettuce.

Coupon number three will say "Purchase a salad dressing and a salad, get $2 off meat," and you find a week in which London Broil is on sale for

$1.99 a pound. Voila! Lettuce, dressing, and meat for free. Pick up a potato for 79 cents and you have a real dinner.

Back at Dollar General Market (a Dollar General with expanded grocery offerings and produce), the disenfranchised are paying $4-$5 for the same thing in what looks like a place you would go to get an MRI, or perhaps dialysis, but certainly not dinner.

If you drove into a neighborhood packed with liquor stores and check cashing establishments, you might roll up the windows and lock the doors, but if you pull into a neighborhood with a Dollar Tree you get excited. Why? What's the difference?

A BRIEF HISTORY OF MIME

The true test of a bargain shopper is how much they remember about all the retail chain stores that have closed in their lifetime. Alexanders begat Old Navy, The Wiz begat Best Buy, and Caldor, Ames and Jamesway begat Target. And if you don't remember Caldor, then you're doomed to repeat yourself.

Caldor was ultimately quite possibly one of the shittiest stores on the face of the earth. It had a khaki/beige color scheme, miserable employees, no service, high prices, out of date technology, much too much security, and an overall look and feel of complete and total failure. It looked like a beige prison that sold plasticware. They were so nuts that I think I recall Sensormatic tags stuck on the ceiling fixtures, just in case someone tried to make a run for it.

For years, customers watched it fall apart until it was ultimately liquidated and closed, just like Sam Goody and Tower Records (USA retail locations, specifically). Educated (and I don't mean in a classroom) customers laughed endlessly at the morons who would still frequent these establishments.

Just about a year ago, I remember browsing a Sam Goody and watching someone purchase blank audio cassettes for some outrageous price like $14 for a package of four. Hopelessly stuck in the past, these Luddites kept the chain in business well past its expiration date.

In exchange, Sam Goody still stocked blank audio cassettes, right next to limited edition incense burners. They even had a frequent shopper program that you had to *pay to join*. I often referred to their "Replay" membership program as "The Luddite Card," and none of the employees got the joke, which was a good part of the problem.

They knew who their customers were and they beat them until they all died or went deaf. If Bee Gees records were available in Braille, they'd still be selling them right now.

For the last few years if you even saw a teenager purchasing anything in a Sam Goody you wanted to find their parents and send them for drug testing.

My grandmother shopped at Sam Goody. If she were not in assisted living and had they not gone under, she would still be shopping there. I haven't purchased anything at Sam Goody that didn't have a 75% clearance tag on it in at least ten years.

But let's get back to you and your stuck up attitudes about how you buy soda. Do you want to be the grandmother or grandfather who still shops at Radio Shack? Okay, I hear you saying "Now what's wrong with Radio Shack?" We can deal with that later. Next time you go to Radio Shack, try to find a customer under the age of 50. You need to evolve in your shopping or things will just continue as they are. Chances are you pay more for two cases of soda than I got paid to pour four cases down the drain.

I already hear the excuses: you don't like to mail in rebates, they never send you a check. You don't clip coupons because it's too much work. There's too much involved to get a good discount, you're too busy/tired/disorganized. Want to know why? *Cause you drink too much soda, stupid!* Go outside and take a walk around the block, then drink a glass of water, after which you won't be so overwhelmed by the challenging task of mailing out an envelope.

Coupon shoppers always talk about frequent shopper clubs, like the aforementioned Sam Goody one. We all have shoeboxes full of these things, everything from movie theaters, to rental car companies, to the BBOC (Beanie Babies Official Club).

But every once in a while you hit a club that is both useless and annoyingly heavy-handed with the solicitations and one such place is a restaurant that shall go unnamed. One night, in the middle of nowhere, I stopped in the restaurant and I filled out the membership card agreement.

The program gave me points for dining, and three years later I am still unable to find out what exactly the points can be redeemed for. Every single day for the better part of three years I got an email from the restaurant telling me what the specials were that evening. The restaurant is more than 500 miles from my home and the food was awful.

No doubt I would have forgotten its very existence and the bad dining experience, but I am reminded every single day. The only humor in it for me is that when I think about how bad it was, I imagine how outrageous it that is they offer some of these foods at all. When you're eating at a gas station on the highway you don't want to order the fish special.

There is another annoying kind of marketing which, unfortunately, can work wonders, and that is the "trust us blindly, we're young/hip/cool and very smart!" We used to have a chain here in New York called The Wiz, which was an electronics store with the usual assortment of music, video-tapes, and video games. Well, before that we had a chain called Crazy Eddie which offered great service and values until one of its owners (Eddie Antar) was found guilty of stock fraud and then fled the country (he later returned to stand trial, was sent to prison, and ultimately released. A year later he attempted to revive the brand with a website, it folded three years later. Sam Antar, another co-founder of Crazy Eddie, now runs whitecollarfraud.com.)

The Wiz was a simple store: 90 percent of the inventory was overpriced garbage, and the other 10 percent was extremely overpriced garbage. Sales tactics at The Wiz worked like this: whatever the customer says or thinks, convince them they are wrong until they buy something.

Nobody at The Wiz ever had a clue what was popular or why. Near the end, when you could buy a VCR for $50 everywhere, The Wiz would try to pretend DVD hadn't come out yet and were still trying to charge $250 for all the old stock of VCRs they had left. Any time a pathetically bad new technology would come out, The Wiz would load up on it to an extreme, then try to sell it at full price, all the time trying to convince the customer he "needed" to buy the product simply because it was cool if The Wiz was pushing it. When the technology would tank, instead of liquidating the inventory, it would rot on the store shelves for years still marked up at full price.

Some of the great Wiz failures included pre-recorded 8mm videocassettes, the Phillips CD-I system, Sony Minidisc, and 3-D video glasses. Some trends caught them completely by surprise. The store often didn't have these products for a year after their introduction—CD-R drives, Sony Playstations, and region-free DVD players.

Everyone who worked at The Wiz was so full of themselves. After all, this was the culture which was encouraged to believe the company was as cool and cutting edge as they claimed to be. It was a miserable failure in the end. First, they tried expanding out of New York state; I remember the store in Massachusetts very well.

The folks in Massachusetts were so put off by the arrogant staff that the store was a ghost town within weeks of opening. When they finally went out of business, there was a sigh of relief. You could almost picture the newly laid-off wondering what went wrong. How could a store so big and great go out of business? And that in itself was some bizarre form of poetic justice.

Tower Records had sort of become the same thing: while the staff at Tower was never anywhere near as obnoxious as that of The Wiz, the product itself didn't merit the prices and overall feel of the store. For example, Tower Records retail stores in the United States basically ignored the existence of the iPod.

Sure, they sold them after a couple of years, once it was unavoidable, but for a long time you could walk in and see the price of $17.99 for a CD you could purchase on iTunes for $9.99.

There had been several years when people were illegally downloading this very same music. Did Tower sell blank CDs when they first appeared? No. And when they finally did sell them, it was at such a high price you would have been better off just buying the overprice pre-recorded CDs at Tower.

Tower rested on its laurels. Why they thought any self-respecting adult would show up at 3:00 p.m. on a weekday and wait on line for two hours to see a musician play an in-store performance of four songs I don't know. If all the kids were bootlegging the music and they needed the adults to keep paying for it, in-store performances were not going to make any difference.

Just to stay hip they started selling a lot of collectible toys and action figures. Tower did these insane deals for exclusive product lines of these toys. Again, what self-respecting adult is going to pay $30 for a plastic action figure of Jim Morrison? Even if you were the biggest Doors fan in the world, what the hell are you going to do with this thing? Hold it over the chickens you sacrifice in your living room every full moon? Let's face it, these items had very limited appeal. The fact that no one at Tower thought they had such limited appeal pretty much says it all.

Back around 1987 I remember my father taking me to Tower Records in downtown Manhattan, and I remember exactly *how cool* it seemed. As if it were the coolness center of the universe at that very moment, with its neon zigzag patterns, different floors with different kinds of music, and of course the biggest selection of Cassingles (single songs sold on cassette, a format intended to replace 45s but never quite took off) I had ever seen. At any moment, Michael J. Fox might have popped in to buy a record. It was all terribly exciting.

By the time I was an adult and could go to Tower Records whenever I liked, they still had the "Hip Hop" section in the basement, but they had begun struggling to sell imported CD singles by Gina G for $11.99. There were cassettes that rang up at $18 and when you actually bought one they usually snapped on the first play since they had been on the shelf for so long. To their credit, there was a Tower clearance outlet, which was still extremely cool, but it closed in the '90s, and Tower Video became a laughing stock after DVDs were introduced. This was a real shame because in the '80s (and the early '90s) they were really cutting edge with their laserdisc selection.

Regardless, the core business was stale. It had turned into The Wiz—"trust us blindly because we're cool." I'm not sure if this is better or worse than what it has evolved into, which is just blatant lying through ignorance, throwing around words that don't belong together in an attempt to confuse the customer.

Or maybe I am giving too much credit to the lobotomized morons who work in electronic chains today; perhaps they really think they sound credible and intelligent to the customer (and often, they do), but in the end if you know what you're talking about you need two Tylenol before setting foot in an electronics big box store today.

Here's the ultimate example in bad customer service, the one where it actually could have cost someone their life. Kmart was going out of business and I went to go check out the liquidation sale. My whole thing with liquidation sales is to check out the perimeter of the store where the merchandise has not been picked over as much.

Anyway, I walked past the gun case and it was unlocked and open. There was an open box of shotgun shells with a couple missing. Above it were the shotguns, unlocked, just sitting there. Mind you, the liquidation company was running the store now, not Kmart.

The employees on property were working for the liquidation company, as most of the Kmart employees had just been laid off. The store was crowded with people. I completely panicked. First, I ran and grabbed Jean by the arm and explained. We ran to the front of the store and were shouting at the customer service people to listen to us, but they couldn't have cared less.

Why should they care? They were going to be out of work in a couple of days. In that situation I didn't have the patience or the bad sense to stand there and explain to them the whole scenario. "Are you not concerned someone who just lost their job might want to do harm to someone still working here or perhaps try to hold up the store?" You see, when you deal with this bad customer service, you need to explain everything a dozen times, and in a very time-sensitive situation like that there is no opportunity to do so.

Luckily, nothing happened, but it was a real eye opener. If there is ever a life-threatening emergency the last place I want to be is in a big box retail store. Need proof? Check out a Wal-Mart in New Orleans.

Meanwhile, back at Tower Records, the liquidation sale is in full swing. I stopped in just to see if there were any deals and, lo and behold, there were not. But you know what they do have is the token bad customer who walks into a store loaded with neon-colored signs that say "GOING OUT OF BUSINESS" "EVERYTHING MUST GO," "50 PERCENT OFF ENTIRE INVENTORY" and then asks for a new release. When they are told that it is not in stock ask if they can special order it. I've been to hundreds of liquidation sales and I have seen it every single time. Like a good party trick, it never fails to entertain.

BENIHANA

Employee ignorance and indifference exists anywhere in retail, not just at electronics and record stores. One of my favorite examples of this is in restaurant "frequent diner" programs.

Waitstaff are doing just that, waiting on customers. Customer orders food, waiter / waitress brings food, customer eats food, waiter / waitress stops by and says "how is everything?" customer nods with mouth full, waiter / waitress stops by and says "any dessert?" customer grabs stomach and grasps for air, says "no thanks, just the check," waiter / waitress brings check, customer pays. Pretty simple, right?

Well, restaurants are not about food anymore, now they're "entertainment experiences."

Millions of dollars in research and development into color schemes, fonts and layouts of menus, music selection—all that comes down to a bottleneck with the waitstaff.

You see, if you set it up just right the customer is supposed to have the intended experience, but invariably the waiter/waitress is either left out of the loop or is not qualified to deliver the performance as intended. The most glaring example always takes place when you use some kind of frequent diner card.

Take the example of Benihana Emperor's Club. Benihana in itself is a fascinating trainwreck these days. When you're paying $100 for dinner in an "authentic hibachi restaurant," which is anything but authentic since you're probably sitting in a strip mall outside Phoenix, as opposed to Osaka, you want a good show.

Not to sound racist, but nothing can ruin the good show like having an Indian or Mexican hibachi chef. I'm quite positive that both Indian and Mexican people are perfectly capable of making dinner on a hibachi. I'm sure that both Indian and Mexican people are perfectly capable of doing so in a friendly and fun way. What Indian and Mexican people are not perfectly capable of being is a Japanese man in a big red chef's hat telling awful jokes in an authentically bad Japanese accent.

Since we are paying for a show, we should have the right actors for the parts. If you're trying to tell me that I am paying $100 just for the food, then why the hell do you care what color the ceiling is and what music is playing?

Speaking of the music, last time we went to Benihana they were playing Beyonce and Coldplay. I love Coldplay, but somehow it didn't seem authentic at all. I know that my expectations are high for a restaurant whose entrance is adorned with color photocopies of photographs of the owner posing with D-list celebrities at parties, but I'm just saying, if your R&D company told you that "X&Y" fit the bill for an "authentic Japanese hibachi restaurant," you got taken. I want to hear that ding ding ding with some kind of pan flute or—who knows what? Play that music which sounds like someone screaming because a car just ran over their foot or, at the very least, play some Japanese pop music. Let's complete the "entertainment experience" properly, shall we?

Benihana introduced a frequent diner's card called "The Emperor's Club," which ran on a simple points system. Every time you dined, you presented the card and earned points. When you had earned enough points, you were given a gift certificate for a future purchase.

While it may be simple enough for you and me to follow, it was far too complicated for their staff, who royally screwed it up on every occasion. I personally witnessed people who flipped out and had their whole show ruined when the staff wouldn't go along with the program's rules. One time I saw a guy scream at the restaurant manager and he had an actual printout of the Terms & Conditions with him, but after a long argument the manager admitted he couldn't read in English. I have trouble believing he was really the manager, but there you are. No matter what the real story was you would never get it out of them.

The real story is always the same in these sorts of retail disputes: the staff simply does not know how to do whatever it is you expect them to do. Excuses and made-up rules go flying, but you must stick to this principle— they simply do not know how.

REGURGITATE AND REPEAT

So far we've just been looking at how we eat in and around retail environments; we haven't even begun talking about other ways we spend our money. I don't say these things to insult anyone who either works at or frequently dines at these restaurants. All I want is for more people to step back and look at the situation from my perspective and then go out and see whether they agree or disagree so that they may be more objective in their purchasing decisions. Most people don't see that casual dining is nothing more than show business and you need to understand what you're spending your money on. I have faith in the human race that once people understand better, things will change.

Most of my anger towards bad service comes out at chain restaurants where so much is built up and then the service or food is lackluster and instead of apologizing and making it right, they basically tell the customer to pay. When you're paying $12 for a hamburger, everyone in the place should be kissing your ass and begging you to come back. But they don't. They act as if they are doing you a favor and you should be kissing their ass for the privilege. Then they scatter, mumbling into their headsets, presumably because the planes need to land.

This probably won't come as a surprise, but I'm sure your local diner charges $3-$4 for a bigger hamburger and they are always happy to see you when you come in. Don't misunderstand me: I like theme restaurants and chain restaurants very much, but I like them in an extremely ironic and dark way. If you think you won't find me at a Chili's watching the parade of human failure you're wrong.

In entertainment, when the material being presented is of a sub-standard quality, the director or producer may opt to incorporate gimmicks. A popular gimmick in theater is the act of putting a "plant" in the audience, someone who laughs and applauds at designated times in order to encourage other members of the audience to do the same. If you're unsure if the show is worthy of applause, you may be subconsciously tricked into applauding, and thus, as a crowd begins to applaud, the applause grows as more and more people are tricked into applauding based on the larger number of people who are already applauding. You believe that the show must be good if so many other people are applauding. The trick almost always works.

RED LOBSTER

I will not comment on the quality of the food at Red Lobster, but just say that they employ a number of gimmicks. Next time you're with a group of people, bring up Red Lobster. Many will say they never eat there, they would never eat there, or they ate there once and they hated it. However, one person will always be extremely passionate about it, rambling on incessantly about how wonderful it is. When you ask them what they eat there, the answer is almost always the same—the rolls. The breadbasket of butter-and-cheese soaked biscuits is the draw, but those are free. You could go in and order a soda and get unlimited refills of the bread. Walk around a Red Lobster and look at all the unfinished plates going in the trash because the customers are stuffed with three baskets of rolls.

One of my favorite things these restaurants do is make up faux holidays. "Lobsterfest" is the best: lobsters are the same price as they normally are all year long. There is no real reason to celebrate. One would assume that the celebration stems from the month that Red Lobster determined they sold the fewest lobster dinners every year and needed a gimmick to boost sales. Let's pretend you came here from another planet, saw the signs, and heard the commercials.

You might be led to believe that people send each other "Happy Lobsterfest" greeting cards and engage in ceremonial rituals around it every year. That is usually the premise for my ritual each year, which is to send "Happy Lobsterfest!" greeting cards to my friends. Occasionally I will call them and ask what they are doing for Lobsterfest this year, or perhaps in November call Red Lobster locations and ask whoever answers the phone, "Did you have a good holiday. Did all of your family travel to be with you?"

If marketing firms really believe people are so stupid as to play along, it can be a great deal of fun to actually play along, because that way you will appear to be completely crazy, and the marketers will think twice next year to avoid the barrage of craziness from the previous year. At the same time, it also makes the marketers feel more powerful than they are and that can be a bad thing.

You can't win, but you can have a great time demanding to sit at the fish-shaped table, and when they have run out of Mardi-Gras beads that come with the Lobsterita, you can insist it is religious blasphemy and demand to see a manager! When the whole event is made-up bullshit, it is your duty as a consumer to hold them to it one hundred percent of the way through to the end. It takes a true patron of the casual dining establishment to hold a Lobsterita up to such high standards.

People-watching is always fun, but it's always ten times more fun when they're all miserable. Nowhere on Earth—and I mean nowhere on Earth—will you see people as truly miserable as they are in casual dining restaurants. When you see pictures of children starving to death in Ethiopia, sure, they are really, truly miserable. But those children have no choice in the matter: they are condemned to die and everyone around them is clearly condemned to die as well, as they are all in it together. Can you then imagine that the people who appear even more miserable than the starving children, American adult casual dining consumers, actually *chose* to come to this establishment and spend money?

So why do these people choose to patronize these establishments? Ten years ago, many of these establishments didn't even exist. The most frequent question asked of these patrons who spend fortunes at casual dining restaurants and then complain about it is, "Why don't you just cook?"

WHY DON'T YOU JUST COOK?

How and when did an entire generation grow up not only not knowing how to prepare food for themselves, but believing that paying someone else to prepare food for them was an acceptable everyday occurrence?

People say that in wealthy neighborhoods, customers demand service. The concept is that the customer is wealthy because they work so hard all week and cannot concentrate on "smaller" things, like how they piss away their wealth.

There is also a common misperception that wealthy people eat out in restaurants more than others. I have not found this to be true at all. What I find is that wealthy people have the time and money to learn how to cook, something most people don't have. Most of us are so bad at cooking that we sit around eating fast food takeout while watching "celebrity chefs" on television prepare gourmet food none of us will ever make. We have all caught ourselves saying "wow, they are really talented!" when we are just watching them on TV, unable to taste whatever it is they are making. This is not an accident.

First off, pretty much everyone thinks they can cook. You must have a friend who tells you what a great cook they are, and then when you try their cooking it becomes apparent that they like to play in the kitchen, but they really have no clue what they are doing. Then you have to lie and tell them how great it all was, which only puts in motion a never ending cycle wherein they expect you will want to come over for dinner again, or worse, bring you things they have made at random times.

Some people have this need to feel able in the basic human need of preparing food; others may simply be imitating and idolizing the "celebrity chefs," like all those women on South Beach in Miami who emulate Paris Hilton's every nuance. None of them ever wants to be Paula Dean, the only one whose show is truly enjoyable and entertaining.

The rest of us try to follow instructions carefully. But when you're done trying to make whatever it is, you're so frustrated and have spent so much money on little things you didn't own (since you don't usually cook), that you end up with a big expensive mess which would have been cheaper and easier to simply pay for in a restaurant.

We've all been stumped by random things like "lemon zest," "coriander," measurements like "a pinch," verbs like "drizzle" or, worse, when there is no direction on how to use the ingredients. Somehow these problems don't seem so unique that I am the only person to have found a zester wrapped under the Christmas tree.

When you start to get really hungry in the middle of making whatever it is then you have to have the whole argument with yourself: do I go eat something else now, since I'll go nuts if I have to wait much longer to eat? Then I can have this dish cold later on. But I put all the work into it, and I'll be pissed if I then have to eat it cold. I don't even know how much longer it will take to make. Fuck it, I'll eat now, then I'll stuff myself when this is done. Fine.

Afterwards, when your dish is a total disaster, you lick the plate clean anyway to get your money and effort's worth. And that's just before you feel really sick because you prepared it wrong and your body is not meant to digest a whole bottle of molasses or whatever you used too much of.

You can do what I've done and take it a step further by putting the DVD player in the kitchen to try to "cook-along" with the TV show step-by-step, but this leads to almost certain failure. You end up looking like Donald Duck with a spatula up your ass, an alarm clock wrapped around your head, screaming and yelling at passing cars while your home burns down behind you.

So what's the solution? To dine out more frequently? Well that's unaffordable too, unless you plan on eating hot dogs at 7-Eleven three times a day, and who hasn't considered that a viable option at some point in their life?

CHICKEN MALAISE IS NOT A REAL DISH

Back at T.G.I. Friday's, people in the free world with disposable income are pissing it away on what, in my opinion, is bad food, bad atmosphere, bad service, and uncomfortable furniture. They should know better, they do know better, but they beat themselves up over and over and over again. It is the purest form of human failure I can imagine and in that I have a perverse delight in people-watching. Some people prefer to watch men who go to Hooters to meet women and cannot figure out why they're permanently single.

It is that same mindset that you see in full force at the warehouse clubs, the department stores, and the super centers. This concept of buying things to improve yourself and your life is pure failure. The never-ending shit-sprawl (I know it's crude, but really, is there any other word?) of meaningless product, the movement of that product, and the ultimate disposal of the product for no good reason other than human failure is in itself what it means to live in a "consumer-driven" economy. Do people on anti-depressants shop less? Obviously not, as anti-depressant use goes up every year along with retail sales. Mel Gibson on a real bender would probably suggest that it's a conspiracy that pharmacies are located inside warehouse clubs.

There are so many people who don't even know where to go in order to buy a specific thing. How is it with all the insane combinations of retail stores out there, every one of us gets asked on a regular basis, "I need to buy a _____. Where do you think I should go for that?"

My answer is always the same—"a psychiatrist."

STRIKE A POSE

I often get asked why I think it is so hard to get good service these days. To this my standard reply is always, "You asked for it!" The person then replies, "I didn't ask for anything." And then I nod and say, "Uh huh, that's what I said, you asked for it." There's usually a long pause and some eavesdropping dickhead usually pipes up with "Who's on first?" It would be great to tell you this is a rare occurrence, but it happens several times a day.

Think of an item you purchase on a frequent basis.

Think of how you want the sale to go.

Now think of how the sale gets done the wrong way each time.

PART UN — BITTIES

When I was a kid I liked the Double Bacon Cheeseburger Deluxe at Burger King, without mayonnaise. Burger King had this slogan about how they would make any burger exactly the way you wanted. The old Burger Kings also had microphones at each cash register, so the cashier could tell the short order cook exactly how you wanted your hamburger. No matter how I said it, what time of day I went, anything, the hamburger ALWAYS came with mayonnaise on it, and I would optimistically sit down to eat it and get very disappointed. After this, I would go back to the cash register and ask them for another one without mayonnaise, which I then had to stand and wait for, so that when I returned to the table my mother was finished with lunch and I was just starting. This went on for years. Had the hamburger come with nothing on it and there been a self-service counter for me to make it any way I liked, I would have counted my blessings.

I have bad stomach problems and the bacon double cheeseburgers didn't help much. I used to have trouble drinking a whole glass of water since I was nauseous all the time. To make sure I was drinking water, the glass itself became my unit of measurement. When waiters would come by to fill the water glasses, I would have to ask each time for them to refrain from filling my water glass, but of course they were worried about having their boss think they were not doing a good job.

This ended up in some bizarre altercations, the most memorable of which involved me saying "No more water, please," then placing my hand over the glass, followed by the waiter pouring the water over my hand until the glass was not only full, but the entire table was flooded and everyone's dinner ruined. Thankfully, due to senility, my grandfather still blames my grandmother for that one. I guess time really does heal all wounds.

Every morning at Dunkin Donuts the cashier would ask if I wanted my coffee in the bag with my donuts and every morning I would say no. And then every morning, she would put the coffee in the bag with the donuts and it would make a big mess. In retrospect, maybe I should have walked in one morning with a sign around my neck that said "asshole" but hindsight is everything.

There were a few bad mornings where I just flipped out because, let's face it, $3 for coffee and donuts is a lot of money, and if you're going to ask if I want a hot, wet and sticky wax paper bag to spill all over my desk, generally my answer would be "no." If I worked as a pornographer, it would probably still be "no," but you never know what people are into.

That was almost ten years ago, but things have not really changed all that much in some places. Recently I stopped at a McDonald's at a highway rest stop for breakfast. I ordered a Sausage McMuffin and a small coffee. This was a Sausage McMuffin with no egg. If you read the McDonald's menu it included both—Sausage McMuffin and Sausage McMuffin with egg.

Common sense suggests that you should not have to say "no egg" each time, since the sandwich should not come with egg unless you specify you want it. Yes, I am arguing semantics over a McDonald's breakfast menu, but I didn't write the thing, they did, so I am only following the structure they put in place. Now it doesn't matter if you say "no egg" or not, it always comes with egg. I hadn't ordered one of these things in a good five years, but it still happens.

The tricky thing with the newer McDonald's registers is that you can't see what the order has been placed for or how much per item you're being charged until after you have paid and are given a receipt. There is no screen on the register to show you which items you're purchasing and at what price.

In this case, I was charged for a Sausage McMuffin with egg and given a Sausage McMuffin without egg. There is roughly nineteen cents difference between the two. For a variety of reasons I will explain later, I paid for my McMeal with my American Express card. Taking a good look at the ignorant teenagers working there, I knew it would be nearly impossible to get a nineteen cent refund and I didn't trust them not to spit on my food in return for the hassle. Plus, there was a bigger motivator—I was starving.

Who knows how many McDonald's there are in the world? Looking it up would require me to switch screens and lose this great momentum we have here, so let's just make up some figures and pretend they are real. Is it possible that every day half a million people around the world have the same experience at McDonald's as I did? That half a million unwanted eggs are thrown away by ravenously hungry customers to the tune of $95,000 in sales? If so, McDonald's should look into throwing out soda next because they could really boost their margins.

You see, the point here is the upsell: on our figures McDonald's would make an extra $95,000 a day simply by *ignoring* their customers. Nobody wants to look like a maniac demanding a nineteen-cent refund. Nobody wants spit in their food. The nineteen cents is practically a protection racket.

There have been many environmental- and health-related books and articles written about companies like McDonald's, and I do NOT want you to confuse my banter with any of that. While those people may have various points and opinions, I will not judge you or dictate to you where and what you should be eating. My only point here is the profit they have found by *ignoring* the customer, by doing the polar opposite of "the customer is always right."

If a company like McDonald's is doing this, you better believe many other companies have noticed and followed suit. That is half of the answer to the aforementioned question about why it's so hard to get good service these days. Because it's profitable. If big box retailers gain enough market share, eventually they will just remove the customer-service counters from their stores, since they are the least profitable square footage aside from the restrooms, which many stores already have eliminated.

PART DEUX — L.L. BEAN

Let's look at the abuse of customer service. Once upon a time stores did have decent customer service and offered things like "lifetime returns" on certain products. L.L. Bean being the perfect example of a problem in which people would visit the flagship store in Maine to return clothing they had purchased five or ten years prior and worn consistently until it no longer fit or had rips and stains. Then they would simply bring it back for an exchange. It was not one or two people, but a steady stream. I heard stories about this issue from just about everyone I knew who visited their store.

It reminded me of this "get the guns off the streets" kind of thing Target had sponsored down in Florida, in which you could exchange weapons, no questions asked, for a Target gift card in the amount of $100 or $200. Sounds like a good system, right? Target gets free advertising, helps get illegal weapons out of the hands of people who might use them for harm, whatever. On paper it sounds like a good idea.

But it's just like all of these ideas; they're created by people who are looking at the end result and not thinking about who will show up. Down in Florida, if you're involved with guns at all, you know how easily you can purchase a gun for under a $100. There were *tons* of speculators who went out in advance and bought up every sub-$100 gun they could find and then brought them over to cash in for a huge profit in Target gift cards, some paying 50 cents on the dollar for them. Meanwhile, the potential criminals kept their weapons and the police determined the event a complete success, based on the record number of weapons that were turned in.

The two are related because they both include such naive blind faith. Yes, you should believe that people are good and mean well, but generally not when illegal guns and money are involved.

These things happen in a variety of legal forums. Recently in California driving while talking on a handheld cellphone became illegal. The fine if you're caught is $20 for the first offense. A website that sells cellphone accessories ran a promotion that if you were caught and issued a summons, they would give you a free Plantronics headset with a suggested retail price of $150. You can only imagine what joy the bargain shoppers in California felt when they got pulled over and issued a summons. Can you imagine a promotion which encourages people to break the law and then the absurd nature in which one would have to intentionally stay on the phone as much as possible while driving around trying to get caught breaking the law before the promotion was over?

PART TROIS —

LAST NIGHT A STARBUCKS SAVED MY LIFE

Part three of my "you asked for it" theory goes like this: you like it. That's right, when customer service is removed from the equation it lets people feel "creative." Here's a basic example. There's a coffee shop near a factory down the street. The woman who owns and runs the coffee shop is very attractive; I know this because when we moved to our current neighborhood, all the factory workers would tell me so on a regular basis.

When I finally went to the coffee shop, she was not all that attractive, but she flirted with the factory workers. Behind the counter is a sign listing all of the toppings you can put on your sandwich and a note in cursive writing with hearts over the 'I,' which says simply, "Be Creative!" The factory guys lose it over those two words. They order these fucked up sandwiches with all kinds of things on them and she flirts some more, "Wow! How original!" They brag to each other about how much she liked their sandwich topping combinations. None of them pays attention to the fact that $7.00 for a turkey sandwich is an outrage. Meanwhile, the two guys with a deli three blocks away that has cheaper and better-quality food cannot figure out why business is always so bad.

While it's no secret that men's penises are responsible for lots of bad purchases, sometimes it's the need to avoid confrontation that feeds it as well. When Starbucks first opened, I hated their coffee. The drinks were too strong, too expensive, and too pretentious. Two dollars for a cup of coffee is more expensive than gasoline.

After a few months, however, I found myself at Starbucks every morning. Why? Because I didn't have to get in the "Don't put the coffee in the bag!" argument with them, since they don't have any bags. If I was in a bad mood and didn't want to say whether I wanted cream or sugar, I didn't have to. We all have stories about ordering a Small, Medium, or Large and having them say "Venti" "Grande" and "Tall" back to us, but they put up with it, not us. Besides I could usually get a laugh by saying "For $2 you better put all three in there!" (For what it's worth, when you do that joke in New York you have to word it as "Put all them motherfuckers in there!" or it falls flat.)

However you look at it, it was a liberating experience. True there were no donuts and the coffee was awful, but it was bribery. I was paying more in order NOT to have an altercation first thing in the morning and a lot of people followed suit. Now when you walk in Dunkin Donuts they are so desperate for an upsell that the cashiers sound like used car salesmen. "Coffee. Large. Milk, no sugar! You want motor oil just ninety-nine cent more? Change windshield wiper?"

YOU SPENT YOUR SUBPRIME MORTGAGE MONEY ON CHEESECAKE?

I am hearing about this new trend all over the country now that certain areas are "coming up," that entire towns are "revitalizing," that wealthy people are "moving in." You hear lines like "there are two-million dollar homes." As my friend Carrin says, they are called "two-million" dollar homes because once you have paid an adjustable-rate mortgage, taxes, maintenance and fees on it, over time any slum in North America would end up costing about $2 million. More to the point, the next time you hear about $2 million homes, you should patiently wait to see someone actually PAY $2 million for one of them.

The "our town is special," "our town is going places," "our town is coming up in the world" phenomenon of bullshit stems from two things. First, Americans always wants to feel special. As a Norwegian friend of mine once pointed out, every diner in the country advertises "The Best Pancakes in Town!" on their menu. "Try our world-famous all-American Burger!" If every dump that claimed to be world-famous was truly world-famous then tourists from other countries wouldn't be storming Denny's and IHOP every morning as if it were a pilgrimage to Roy Rogers' grave itself.

The second factor in the "our town is special" phenomenon can be traced to one single franchise of casual dining restaurant—The Cheesecake Factory. I propose that globalization no longer be called globalization.

Instead, I think we should start calling it the CFE or "Cheesecake Factory Effect."

Think of local "family restaurants" and diners, fast food restaurants, all the small-town food establishments you remember from your childhood. Remember how awful most of them truly were, but how you enjoyed them because they reflected your town? Remember how you knew the person who worked behind the counter for most of your life?

Never been to a Cheesecake Factory? Let me describe it for you.

You walk into what looks to me like someone ate a truckload of marble and glass, washed it down with a can of beige paint, and then had a massive case of architectural diarrhea which they then tried to clean up with mirrors. It belongs in a bad movie about New York City. The design looks like someone with too much money and too much ambition decided to open a front for a mafia operation in a B-movie made in the '80s.

Let's see what doesn't work with this image, which should include a room full of patrons in tuxedos and evening dresses.

Upon entering any of these restaurants on any given evening you will first encounter several obese people sitting on benches or chairs, holding large, square coasters that vibrate when their table is ready. The idea of the coaster pager is to place your drink on it, but none of them are drinking anything, and you can't get near the bar, which we will discuss in a minute.

The obese people on benches are usually surrounded by large groups of screaming children, who would be just as happy eating deep fried chicken lips and asshole nuggets at the fast food restaurant across the parking lot as they play games trying to "kill" each other or passively sit on the floor playing video games. The parents are often sweating and screaming at the children to stop doing whatever it is they are doing. The children, who are starving and have plummeting blood sugar levels, proceed to act more violently or more however-it-is they are acting.

You pass this cesspool of human failure and approach the "host's" desk. It's amazing, wherever you go in this country the "hosts" at these restaurants look completely out of place, are almost always female, and you wonder how they have time to work between taking cigarette breaks, drinking all night, and dealing with all the "drama" between them and the bartenders. They are dressed like they are about to attend a board meeting at a big company in a scene from a porno film.

You say something innocuous like "Hello, we would like a table for two, please."

The response always seems the same to me, anywhere you go, any time of day or night. "We are telling people right now there is a 45-minute to a one-hour wait." You don't dare ask how they came up with this number for fear they will intentionally make you wait longer.

If you didn't already know you were not really in New York City, they won't accept a tip for giving you the next available table for fear of being fired. In New York City if you want to get the next available table at a restaurant (with perhaps a few exceptions), just slip the maitre d' a twenty and you will be seated in no time. However, in Bumfuck, Oakladokley, the hostess wouldn't dare jeopardize her precious job handing out pagers for fear that it could cripple her social status. Twenty dollars could never possibly repair the potential damage to her image should she get fired for treating one customer differently from another. I don't have statistics on how many Cheesecake Factory hostesses end up working as prostitutes after their illustrious careers are cut short, but I have a feeling it's pretty high.

At this point, I personally start stalking people sitting at the bar and try to get a table as soon as one is open. This is usually a contest of sorts whereby you see many men circling the bar like sharks, diving at the seats, sometimes before the people leaving have finished standing up. This is sometimes followed by sitting for another 20 minutes at a table covered with someone else's dirty dishes waiting for service.

When you actually do wait the "45 minutes to one-hour" you will discover the wait is 30 minutes or less. Unless of course you're asking for a table for yourself, your bitter spouse, and your eight offspring, which would put you back at the pit of failure near the entrance.

When you're seated, the menu is the size of a small novel. There is little variation in the dishes, but they are given lots of different names. For example, pasta with one kind of sauce is given one name and the same dish with shrimp thrown in is given another name. Then under the "seafood" heading, it seems like the same dish with shrimp is listed again under a third name. When you ask the server what the difference is, they look at you like you're stupid, and how are you ever going to make it here in the "big city" acting all ignorant like that?

Alternately, when you sit down, the server asks you a question like "Have you guys been here before? Do you know how this works?" to which I usually reply "I order food, you bring it, I eat it, and then I pay you? Am I missing something?"

The food is all the same: if you like butter and, statistically speaking I think you do, everything just tastes like they have a cow in the back hooked up to an aerosol hose and they just spray everything with 20 coats of butter in some sort of bizarre culinary sweat-shop operation.

Have you ever seen someone eat something covered in butter and NOT swear it was delicious? Of course not, and so the average consumer thinks that this is "gourmet dining" at its finest. The aforementioned "family restaurant" in town never had a whole menu of martinis, which is just fine because the average customer has never had a martini, either!

Besides the fact that each portion is large enough to feed three people, if you glance over at one of the big families, you will see that each child has a full-sized adult portion in front of them. Forget people who are starving in Africa, there are whole families in a nearby town who could make one of those plates last for a week. You know in advance more than half of the dinner is going right in the trash.

Just like the McDonald's Sausage McMuffin, they are selling you a larger portion at an inflated profit with no interest about whether it will ever be eaten. I don't understand how save the earth type activists can go so postal at cosmetic companies, and I have NEVER seen a protest outside a casual dining restaurant.

So once you're finished and have only eaten half of the food that you have been served, they begin the upsell with dessert. Let's face it, no matter how stuffed you are, after the waiting and the travel, how are you *not* going to order dessert at a restaurant called "The Cheesecake Factory?" How many times a night do people think "Well, that IS what they are known for"? Let's forget the fact that you could have just walked in, bought a slice of cheesecake and left, with no wait. You're here NOW! We MUST live life to its fullest potential!

Alcoholic drama-queen slut-in-dead-end-town hostess, please fetch the 17-year-old part-timer who spends all of his free time fantasizing about you while masturbating instead of doing his homework so he may bring us an outrageously overpriced slice of your finest previously-frozen, shipped-in-from-an-out-of-state factory namesake dessert at once! Ahh, now we are living the good life!

Excuse me, did I call her a slut? I forgot this was a small town what with the big city restaurant and all; I meant to say "popular." Please replace the word "slut" with the word "popular"—thank you. Yes, these are awful stereotypes of people, but you tell me why the hiring policy at these restaurants seems to call for them to play these various roles? Are straight men not capable of writing down people's names, handing out pagers, and telling the customer they have been sentenced to a 60-minute wait?

I venture to say this is the first time that a book about economics has called anyone a slut, and that may be the precise problem here with our economy. How is it that most economists cannot tell you why a restrictor plate race is boring when NASCAR is, on paper, the most financially important sport in our country today?

PUBLIC DISPLAYS OF DESPAIR

Have you ever gotten really sick in one of these restaurants? Not like a cold or a headache, but I mean anything to do with your stomach churning or real pain of any kind? In a privately owned, local restaurant, someone is sure to take notice and offer you assistance. If you're at the table in a diner clutching your stomach, the waiter will notice and offer to help you to the bathroom, or call your spouse, or whatever.

In a casual dining chain, the waitstaff are so busy with their heads up their asses or talking on their headset walkie-talkies, they wouldn't notice if you dropped dead at the table. There is so much noise and such a visual assault that you could in fact be incontinent at the table and no one would ever know.

All of those images and noise are no mistake; they exist to distract you from the food itself, which is always sub-par. They exist so you won't question paying $10 for a hamburger until the next day after you have recovered from your stomach pains. Just like a bad drinking problem, you swear you will never eat there again, but you find yourself there over and over. I know this kind of stasis exists because after you get three or four casual dining chains in one area, people are drawn to them like flies. Once you make a glutton of yourself at them frequently enough for a long enough period of time you realize you have become something of a zombie who ingests fistfuls of saturated fats in exchange for $60 a night.

The Cheesecake Factory in itself is "upscale" as casual dining goes, but remember it's called *casual* dining, not *fine* dining. You still have Chilis, Applebees, Houlihans, Bennigans, T.G.I. Friday's, and a host of other glorified generic diners before you get into your specialty restaurants like Joe's Crab Shack and Red Lobster. No AAA Five-Diamond Award has been given to a Cheesecake Factory and hopefully none ever will be. You won't even find a self-respecting foodie in one. This is in great part due to my theory about why people frequent one casual dining chain over another and that has to do with the "key ingredient."

My theory of the "key ingredient" is this: each chain specializes in making all of their dishes rely on one key ingredient or flavor, so people who are nutritionally deficient in this type of nutrient are inexplicably drawn to that chain. The person does not necessarily like the food, prices, waitstaff or environment, but like the alcoholic they are drawn back time and again.

I have read countless studies that the average American consumer is not properly hydrated, as they consume lots of beverages with caffeine and not enough electrolytes. TGIFriday's "key ingredient" could be salt. Everything tastes like salt to me when I eat there. The consumer, in this case, could be unknowingly drawn to the food at TGIFriday's because their body is craving the salt to help them retain fluids.

Here's another example. Perhaps someone is deficient in Vitamin A, that is to say we know an alcoholic. This deficiency may cause this person to crave dishes which are smothered in butter. Such a person would love Red Lobster, where everything seems to me to come soaked in it.

Maybe it's a sugar rush you're looking for? Bucca di Beppo is for you, a faux-Italian restaurant where everything from the salad dressing to the marinara sauce lists some kind of sweetener, and there's lots of extra glucose-based ingredients in everything. If you request repeatedly, most casual dining restaurants have a book with either basic nutritional information or a list of ingredients. As for the ones that do not, if you insist that you need to know the ingredients for medical reasons, you will be surprised (and perhaps delighted) to be handed a copy of the corporate cookbook, which describes how the food is to be prepared. Once you read these books, you will be horrified.

This theory also helps to explain why certain types of people gravitate towards these restaurants, as their lifestyles result in these nutritional deficiencies in the first place. It's not just that they don't have time to make dinner; for many of the patrons, the artificial environment of the casual dining restaurant is considerably more pleasing than that of their own homes.

Trust me, I know, I've been there. Many of us have walked into a Chili's with some feeling of guilt because as much as we hate the food, as much as we hate the waitstaff, it is considerably nicer than where we are living at the time and the food is better than anything most of us know how to cook. I am not saying that's how I feel about myself and my life at the moment, but when you're 21 in the United States, that's the way life looks. As you know, some people never grow up.

Which brings me back to my question, have you ever gotten really sick at one of these places? Because once you have, not only will you wish you were at that privately owned diner you used to go to, you will realize that your home is much nicer than the restaurant you have been visually and aurally seduced by. When you're really sick and you feel out of your element, you can truly begin to see how cold and awful these artificial environments are. While I don't wish for anyone to get sick, I do wish more people would have this experience so they might have a different perspective before they end up on a bench holding a coaster-pager waiting 30 minutes to pay $10 for a hamburger.

IT IS NOT A VICTIMLESS CRIME

What really hurts is when you see old people seduced by these places. My grandparents used to think Outback Steakhouse was some sort of privately owned restaurant and they would end up there every single night as regulars. First of all, every single night they were made to wait for a table just like everyone else. That would never happen in a privately owned restaurant because the owner would take an interest in serving his frequent customers as well as possible. In a chain, they couldn't care less who you're as long as you pay the check.

Second, my grandmother is a diabetic. She would request all sorts of special substitutions, and the waiters would agree even though they knew that everything came frozen and pre-made in such a way that nothing could really be altered. They were required to ask if she was "allergic" to anything, and since she technically was not "allergic" they would bring her the food she was not supposed to have. So of course she was addicted to the restaurant because when you haven't had real butter in 20 years and you think what you're getting does not have butter in it, but it tastes great, well, you'd go there every night as well!

Watching my grandparents introduce me to the waitstaff was like watching a delusional friend introduce you to the girl he is in love with at a strip club—pathetic and scary at the same time.

As I will talk a lot in this book about bad parenting (because you can't spend as much time in retail stores as I do and not see it) let's discuss the parents who are raising their children on these restaurants. The kids need the experience of the local diners and coffee shops as well. It is unbalanced and unfair to the child to only show them this new mockery of fine dining and not put it in context for them. I'm not one of these conspiracy theory nuts who thinks everything should revert to the way it was in the past and we should shut everything down and go back in time. I simply ask that you put it all in *context*, so that people are free to make their own decisions about how they would like things to be.

IF IT IS SO TERRIBLE, WHY ARE THERE SO MANY OF THEM?

Friendly's was always a mystery to me. Jean, my fiancé, swears by the place, most likely because she has fond memories of her grandmother taking her there as a child. Yes, the ice cream sundaes are good, but they don't hold a candle to a pint of Ben and Jerry's, which didn't exist in Friendly's heyday. The service at Friendly's is notoriously bad. In my experience, you are rarely there without an extended wait and the food is usually of the butter-flavored variety. The prices are "reasonable" when you consider what casual dining prices have become. Regardless, the average Friendly's can be anything but, which is a never-ending source of bad jokes about the chain. They have been in business for a LONG time and you rarely see one going out of business, even in locations with high rents.

That pretty much tells you everything you ever needed to know about us as consumers. A restaurant with mediocre food, mediocre prices, and mediocre service was such a huge success that entrepreneurs were clamoring to start restaurants with positively bad food, bad service, and high prices, since they were just about assured profits beyond their wildest dreams.

In some of the worst (or best, depending on your position) public relations spin I have ever seen, when casual dining revenue took a dip recently, industry spokespeople blamed it on gas prices. Why blame the downturn on the almost intentionally bad service, food, and prices when something completely unrelated (such as gas prices) is so easy a target? Remember that casual dining itself is not a destination; it is almost always attached to a shopping center of some kind.

It's not like their frequent customers all of a sudden learned how to cook at home or were so overwhelmed by all the saturated fats that they were now living in trees, wearing loincloths, and eating Brussels sprouts and assorted flora harvested from the roadsides. And it was said with such confidence, too! "Gas prices," as if they had wasted a dollar on market research.

Even the marketing techniques of casual dining are abysmal. We all knew it was over the top with Olive Garden's "When you're here, you're family" line, as it would certainly be scary to meet an Olive Garden employee who believed this, but what about Ruby Tuesday?

Ruby Tuesday has such notoriously bad food and service that to this day every time we pass one, we have to joke about the time we went there and after waiting 40 minutes for someone to take our order, I said to Jean, "Hey, do you want to go get something to eat and come back?"

Ruby Tuesday's marketing problems go like this: they started issuing coupons and people would show up only to use the coupons and not order anything else. Everyone knows the place is lousy, but if a deal is good enough people will go anywhere. Well, they went in for the loss leader and left. This presumably hurt Ruby Tuesday's profits for a while until they simply decided to stop issuing coupons. Then they had the idea that health-conscious patrons would appreciate seeing the nutritional information on the menu.

You don't need to know how many Weight Watchers points you will need to spend on lunch; all you have to see is the sign above the door and the walls adorned with posters and photographs with picture frames screwed to the wall to know you won't be eating dinner tonight or tomorrow if you want to stay on program. If they were smart they would put cellphone blockers in to keep Overeaters Anonymous members from calling their sponsors.

Recently, Ruby Tuesday began to overhaul all of their restaurants with new interiors, menus, and square plates. Apparently, someone assumed that if the customer received their meal on a square plate that food would subconsciously appear to be better. We decided to check it all out, with the promise I made to Jean that I would buy her a real dinner afterward.

As soon as we walked in, before we were ever seated, they tried to sell us chocolate chip cookies for charity ("Cookies for a Cause"). Why is a casual dining chain with 680 locations holding a bake sale?

I know I'm fat, but they actually sat us at a booth that I literally couldn't fit into. This would seem to go against the goal of attracting people who like to eat at the restaurant. We moved to another table, which gave Jean a nice clear view of the men's room every time someone opened the bathroom door. As part of the interior renovation, they used a paint and color scheme which was designed to attract and highlight fingerprints and condensation in a way rarely seen in casual dining.

My mother always warned me about a day when I would eat in a restaurant and be afraid to even drink a glass of water, and that day had arrived a lot sooner than I expected. My glass had dishsoap in it, so I shared Jean's water with her.

Apparently trying to compete with Red Lobster's "Endless Shrimp," Tuesday was having its "Shrimp Celebration." One of the dishes claimed to be "the perfect storm of texture and flavor." Why did they hire a fourth-grader to write the menu in a book-report style? This didn't stop them from suggesting which wines you could pair each dish with (I wish I were making this up), nor did it stop them from giving us a wine list with prices by the bottle.

On one hand, I respect the fact that a meal like this would encourage most people to drink as much as possible to forget it had ever happened; on the other hand, if you order a bottle of wine at Ruby Tuesday's, there is something very wrong with you.

The aforementioned "perfect storm" didn't actually hit us until about halfway into the meal when we took turns in the bathroom, as we would continue to do for the rest of the evening.

Our waitress had a photocopy of the nutritional information, on which she had written the number of Weight Watchers points per dish. I double-checked her math when I got home and found it to be accurate: the average entrée was a full day's worth of points. This should not be too much of a shock. For example, Jean ordered a turkey burger in an attempt to see what the healthier fare on the menu was like. It came topped with avocado, mayonnaise, bacon, and cheese. Why then they bothered to put it on a whole-wheat bun (or a square plate) can only be read as an attempt to confuse ignorant people into believing they are eating something healthy, when it is quite obvious that they are not.

The family of three at the table next to us were engaging in all the usual cheapskate routines like ordering one salad bar and then having the father go up and get three plates so overloaded that he left a trail of blue cheese on the carpet behind him as he walked back to the table. After they had finished, they strangely ordered three more meals of chicken fingers to go. The waitress brought them an enormous shopping bag, which they proceeded to open in order to inspect each and every chicken finger before putting it back in the bag, paying without tipping, and leaving. After they got up, we noticed a Black & Decker electronic pest repeller plugged into the wall behind them.

With tip our check came to $42, an absurd amount of money for what we received.

When you serve such bad food, charge such high prices, and offer such poor service, you have to rely on the faux-atmosphere, which Ruby Tuesday completely lacks. At this point you can either go out of business or deceive your customers, so Ruby Tuesday simply took the nutritional information off the menu and kept everything at full price with no coupons.

Truth in advertising for restaurants should be simple. Before you dine, you should be allowed to see the employee restroom and make sure that it is clean, that the soap dispenser is full, and that the sinks have hot water. Your food should actually be cooked on site, not just defrosted and reheated.

None of these issues is ever up for discussion in an advertisement; they show just a group of friends getting drunk and eating proprietary snacks like "Winger Zingers" or "Riblets." Next time you see an ad for one of these places on TV look at it carefully: the guys are hanging out, the girls are giggling, and everyone is having "fun," or their impression of it. Next time you're in one of these restaurants, look around—everyone is *fucking miserable*.

You can go to a dialysis clinic and see people smiling and trying to enjoy whatever life they have left, telling jokes as best they can, and trying to have fun in the worst possible situation. And then you have casual dining, where everyone looks like they have just witnessed a nuclear holocaust while waiting patiently for their orders of watered down mixed drinks and salsa-covered entrees. It makes you wonder how else a restaurant can insult customers while taking their money. Don't wonder for too long. You can't even spit in a retail environment without hitting some organized procedure dictated to the employees as a "time saver" for the "customer's benefit," which subversively says, "we couldn't care less" to those very same customers. What follows are some of my favorites.

STICKY PAWS

The first thing is the illogical concept of fountain soda dispensing. This is the most simple proof that to a fast food chain the customer is always wrong. When you order a fountain soda, watch it be filled by the clerk who, instead of holding the cup patiently under the nozzle and waiting for the foam to settle down, and then finally filling the cup, impatiently holds the soda cup under the nozzle and wastes three or four cup's worth of soda by letting it pour over the brim. He then presents you with this cup in a hasty manner that is covered in soda and will require you to wash your hands. We have all had this experience in many different places and it is one of those small flaws which make such a powerful statement. The store employees value their time over yours, even though you're paying for their time. While this used to be considered somewhat acceptable, because of the extremely low out of pocket cost for your meal, now that the prices of fast food meals have become so incredibly high, it is simply no longer acceptable. However, this trend continues nonetheless. I will talk about that more in a minute, but before we leave the fast food establishment, we will explore one more example.

When you order that soda via a drive-thru window, thus paying for convenience, the clerk often hands you the soda and your change simultaneously. That means not only are you going to have to pull over and park to wash your hands, thereby eliminating any real convenience, but you now have soaking wet money which you will have to somehow make a mess of yourself putting back into your pocket or purse. This is another simple red flag that the employee values their time more than yours. In many cases they are instructed to do this by the restaurant in order to keep wait times shorter; the restaurant is basically saying directly to the consumer that your comfort is of no concern to them whatsoever.

D.I.Y. CULTURE HITS
THE GROCERY SCENE

The same thing goes with self-checkout at the grocery store. The first time I saw self-checkout it was like some kind of happening. Star Market on Commonwealth Ave near Boston University had it first. People were lined up to the back of the store to try it, while the registers with actual cashiers were empty. To this day I still remember a townie in line saying "Ring your own groceries? Next thing you know, you're gonna have to stock your own shelves!"

Quartets of teenagers lined up with one item just to play with the machines. It was living history, and you could see research and development people freaking out. You could see the cashiers feeling threatened. Most importantly, you could see the customers basking in the glory of less unpleasant human interaction.

Why is there almost no customer service anymore? You, the consumer, asked for it. It didn't take a survey poll or anything else to prove that to me, it was proved with my own two eyes. For the next couple of years every time another grocery store got self-checkout it was the same thing. I would see lines of people in Shaws, Stop & Shop and just about everywhere. It was nothing short of a cultural revolution.

Walk around a grocery store and watch people at the checkout some day, the miserable looks they give cashiers say it all.

SERVICE AS A WEAPON

Another way in which customer service may be used as a weapon to deter people from expecting it is to employ techniques that make the customer service representative appear to be doing his best impression of Jerry Lewis doing an impression of Helen Keller.

One of the easiest and best examples I can give you is when you're in a store looking for a specific item and you don't see it on the shelf. Reluctantly, you go find a store employee and tell them that you've looked, but the item is not on the shelf, and can they please see if there are any more in the back of the store

The first thing they do every time is walk you right back to where you had been and look exactly where you were looking, but the only thing is they take ten times longer to look for the item than you did in the first place. Usually the next response is that they are sold out. This is why I don't think all forms of violence should be completely illegal.

CALL CENTER ABUSE

We are all familiar with another form of customer service as a weapon, which is the outsourcing of call centers to other countries, who then employ persons with a limited vocabulary in the English language and who often impersonate Americans.

"Hello, this is Scott," says a man with a thick accent.

"Scott, buddy, what's up? How was your holiday weekend? You guys do some burgers on the grill?" is usually my first response. My friend Matt has a good one. In his very dry American accent he says, "Hello Scott, my name is Punjabi. How are you today?"

Once you get past this, the first amount of information they request is then intentionally misheard until you start ripping out your hair and hang up the phone. Do I really need to tell you that we all try to limit our calls to customer service centers now as the direct result of this tactic?

Before this there was the trend of computer attendants answering the phone with endless menus that seemed to loop into themselves so it became literally impossible to get a human being. Many companies have taken to not publishing their phone numbers, leaving people to share this "confidential" information on websites. If a company really wanted to eliminate the problem, they truly would have no phone lines installed. This will never happen because the bloated corporations would then be full of employees who would actually have to show up and do work, instead of making "conference calls" all day and hiding behind their voicemail. As we know, the employees are going to cover their own asses first. This was basically the inspiration for "telecommuting," which means you don't even have to go to work, but can just phone it in.

Might I suggest firing all the leeches and just selling products for a reasonable price to begin with? No, of course not, that would make too much sense, and you'd have to tell me that I don't understand the economy.

SECOND MOVEMENT
"MURDER ON THE SALES FLOOR"

ODOR

Several members of Parliament Funkadelic got into the habit of not bathing while they were recording an album. Many recount sleeping on the floor of the recording studio every night for weeks while recording. The only thing they did was eat, sleep, and record music for the better part of five years.

As part of the ongoing mythology they were creating, the term "funk" was used to describe the odor in the recording studio. Therefore, the worse you smelled, the funkier you were, and thus a behavior that would normally be considered distasteful or antisocial was celebrated as being desirable and as part of the common good. During the mid to late 1970s this kind of thinking among all sorts of organizations seemed quite progressive, propelling the perception of Parliament Funkadelic's artistic integrity into the stratosphere.

Anyone in their right mind would have suggested that a multi-million-dollar recording studio should not be turned over to a dozen or more adults, many of whom were raging drug users and who dressed in diapers and sheets, refusing to bathe, but this is the great thing about the entertainment business—as long as you're generating income for someone, you can have free reign to push the boundaries as far as you please.

While the underlying message of a great deal of the work had to do with civil rights, you have to wonder if certain key members of the civil rights movement were not so horrified by the behavior of these successful public figures as to consider whether they should be representing a similar cause.

I can personally relate to this a great deal. Your average "stay at home mom" who lives in the South wants nothing in the world to do with a loud-mouth Jewish man from New York (a triple negative in their eyes) telling people how to coupon shop. Why do they put up with me? Because I am considerably more entertaining than they are and therefore have the ability to generate a larger audience than they do.

Just as I try, with my routine as a fat guy in a Rolling Stones t-shirt giving grocery store cashiers the finger, to break down the stereotype of a woman who is a mother, does all the grocery shopping, cooking and cleaning for her family, and is therefore responsible for saving money at the grocery store, Parliament was trying to turn the civil rights movement away from serious discussions about equality and demonstrative protests and toward a dance party in outer space. It was a simple, yet powerful idea. You get people of many races to dance together to the same music and they will be less likely to dislike each other for superficial reasons outside of the theater.

It is my hope that we may help to end the stigma that "only poor people use coupons," "only women use coupons" or anything similar.

FREE PUDDING

It is 3:00 a.m. and I am in Staten Island with a car full of pudding.

No, this is not a line from a Beatles song. It's a Sunday night and over in

Pennsylvania, two states away, one grocery chain had put both pudding and deodorant on sale: 10 of each for $10.

A good "10 for 10," as it's commonly known among bargain shoppers, is like crack. This was an especially potent dose, since I had to drive two states away to get it. The pudding manufacturer had recently issued coupons for $10 off the purchase of 10 pudding cups, and there are always loads of $1 off 1 deodorant coupons to be had. This was a virtually unlimited supply of pudding and deodorant, two items which would normally be too overpriced to even consider buying in bulk.

For many years, I was angry every time I ran out of deodorant. I would stare at the store shelves begrudgingly, fighting with myself about whether I *really* needed it because I felt $3 or $4 for it was such an outrageous ripoff. When I began bargain shopping, I started buying it on eBay in bulk, paying about $1 a stick.

One day on a message board, I posted a deodorant deal on Amazon and women all went crazy telling me how to get deodorant for free. We haven't paid since.

Deodorant is one of those staples in coupon shopping. It goes on sale for a dollar, and there are coupons for a dollar off a few times a year, so now I am the one looking at people in stores paying $3 and explaining to them how to stop.

We don't have pudding in the house because it's usually way too expensive for what it is. I don't mean instant pudding; I mean the pre-cooked, ready-to-eat pudding cups. Besides, they are really great for donating to charity, since they don't require refrigeration and people usually donate meal items, not desserts.

So here we are in the car late at night on the Staten Island expressway driving home with a car full of pudding, calling all of my friends and bragging about what a big score it was. All of a sudden, out of the corner of my eye, I saw a sign.

Now when most people tell you they saw a sign they mean they spoke to God, or they are all caught up in one of those stupid M. Night Shyamalan stories that they now think is real. No, I am a down-to-earth person so when I tell you I saw a sign I mean quite literally that I saw an actual sign.

It said "Shop Rite."

Without hesitating I took the next exit and we started looking around the car for our coupons. We both knew and we could smell it a mile away—free cat litter. Cat litter is another one of those items which is outrageously overpriced and it also goes on "10 for 10." In this case we had a fresh batch of $1 off 1 coupons. Fifteen minutes later we were back on the highway with a car full of pudding and a hundred pounds of cat litter (the total cost for the cat litter was about sixteen cents, in case you were wondering).

Yes, there is a perverse joy in filling the car with free merchandise, almost regardless of what it is.

$1/1 ON A TRIAL SIZE

Now I know you're thinking that I must be in a unique area because items like deodorant "never" go on sale for a dollar where you live, but I promise if you keep your eyes on the circulars every week, sooner or later you will see it, and you can buy so much in one visit to the store you'll have enough for a couple of years. But let's pretend you're right and your grocery store does not have such a deal. No problem.

Your drugstore, your big box retailer, and possibly even your local convenience store all sell trial size deodorant for 99 cents. In a majority of cases, the $1 off 1 deodorant coupon will say "good on any size," and when it does, you can simply use the $1 off on a 99-cent item. Okay, so you may feel like you're living in a motel using trial size deodorant every day, but it's much cheaper than paying $3 for it.

The overall concept here is this: charging $3 for deodorant is outrageous, combined with the fact that, as we discussed earlier, the big box retailers are completely insane. You can kill two birds with one stone by using the manufacturers' coupons at the big box retailer to do things like buy 99-cent trial size deodorant with a $1 coupon, so essentially you're getting the things you need on their dime. The manufacturer is paying the retailer, the retailer is recording it as a "sale," and you won't smell so bad. A key factor here is that no actual money is coming out of your pocket, which has very serious economic implications in our "consumer driven economy."

Think about what I am saying to you. This is *one* product and consider how many household products we use. I try to get the manufacturer to pay the retailer for the goods and services I use whenever possible and on many occasions they end up paying me money on top of the freebies.

With this in mind, tell me it isn't amazing that we still are fighting hunger in this country. This is one of the great problems with organized charities. They ask for money and we all donate, and then they spend $3 on deodorant. I'd rather pull up and give them a car full of free deodorant that I paid for with coupons, but most just want money to spend as they "need." Now I'm not saying they don't mean well and that they aren't good causes; of course they do and of course they are, but just because they are charitable causes does not mean that they know entirely what they are doing. I should also stipulate here I am not talking about charities that have to do with medical research, which is a topic I am not qualified to discuss; I am really talking about programs that feed the hungry, for the most part.

Basic supplies such as toothpaste, mouthwash, hand soap, bar soap, dish soap, paper towels, and shampoo are all items that follow the same basic formula. Sooner or later they can be had for around $1 and you can use a coupon for them that is worth around $1.

These are always the items you should start trying to coupon with because they are very simple, you generally always need them, and once you stockpile them you really begin to realize immediate savings and get more comfortable with using coupons properly.

How do you know you're doing it right? When you have more coupons than the store has product on the shelves, then you're doing a good job. If you only need two of something and they are free, you had better buy them all. Donate everything you don't need to charity; to be honest, I usually give some of everything to my friends, and the rest to charity, but you can do whatever you feel is right for you. My point is this: the merchandise will do more good in the trunk of your car than it will on a store shelf where some uneducated consumer might pay actual money for it.

LAUNDERING DISNEY DOLLARS

Real coupon shoppers look for opportunity everywhere. A few years ago on vacation at Disneyland, I realized you could buy "Disney Dollars" with your credit card and then exchange them for real money with no fees or penalties of any kind. I had just received a credit card with 0% interest on all purchases for one year and I earned points on it I could redeem for free gift cards to a variety of merchants. The "Disney Dollars" are considered a purchase and not a cash advance because they are kept as souvenirs. Technically, they are not legal tender and because Disneyland is not the Federal Reserve, it would be impossible for them to call it a cash advance.

Over the course of our vacation, I bought Disney Dollars on the card at every opportunity, earning myself a heavy cash loan with no interest for one year and enough points for a variety of gift cards. The cash could then be deposited into an Emigrant Direct account and I could be paid interest on it for 11 months before returning the principal to the credit card company at no cost. We decided to call this practice "Laundering Disney Dollars." Now it was labor intensive because you can only purchase $50 worth of Disney Dollars at a time, but the customer service people will in fact let you purchase them as many times as you like. While this may seem totally absurd, the truly absurd thing about it is how many people already "launder Disney Dollars" on their vacations as well.

GIFT BASKETS & OTHER VALUE-ADDED BUNDLES

Sometimes retailers think they have got the better of the consumer and I think this is where the term "anarchy" really applies. I was in a grocery store which has a very good house brand of coffee. People like to drive to this place from great distances just to buy some of this coffee, which is intentionally produced in limited quantities to boost demand.

One Sunday we took a drive over there only to discover they had sold out. Now I don't know how you like to grocery shop, but I like to listen to The Clash or The Rolling Stones on my iPod.

So anyway, here we were walking around and I noticed the store was now selling shrink-wrapped gift baskets. The coffee itself is about $8 and the gift baskets contained the coffee and two mugs for about $30. While Mick Jones was screaming something in my ear, I ripped open the sealed gift basket, removed the $8 bag of coffee I had driven there for, and took it to the register to purchase, leaving in my wake a worthless basket with two coffee mugs.

I felt sorry for the employee who had to go in later and redo the entire thing, but she should blame her boss for trying to fleece the consumer. Without question, many other people who showed up to buy that $8 coffee ended up buying the whole overpriced basket they didn't need, but that was not my problem.

If I had been disappointed that the coffee was sold out when I got there, I was downright angry when I discovered they were just essentially trying to scalp it. Luckily for me, they didn't think to put a sticker over the UPC code that read "not for individual sale." Amateurs.

It's no accident that I listen to loud music on my headphones while I shop at these places because when you rip open a gift basket like that you don't want to hear a recently transplanted employee yelling at you, "Sir, you can't do that!" and trying to start some kind of moral argument as if you're shoplifting. I never shoplift; I just wanted to buy the item that I came there to buy at the price set by the store. I think $8 for a pound of coffee is insane, but I do splurge on good coffee. How far can you take the argument with someone whose command of the English language is so limited? How far can you take the argument with a grown man who's only enjoyed indoor plumbing for the last six weeks of his life?

So I usually just keep the tunes going and am intentionally oblivious to those around me. When you look like that much of a moron dancing through the aisles, they just assume you're crazy and don't want to argue with you because they never know if you're just crazy-crazy or crazy-dangerous.

PONS 'N PADS

Shame is a trait which should be reserved for family events. All public places basically require you to be shameless if you wish to be thrifty. Setting aside the bad stereotype of the lazy cashier who does not want to deal with all your coupons and makes nasty comments about how you must be poor—and believe me, you will encounter plenty of those—stores and marketers have figured out how to make you pay just so you will not be embarrassed.

Let's talk about tampons.

Now, this may be a shock to a lot of you, but women have a tendency to menstruate.

Do you have *any* idea how much easier it would be to get along in this world if more people just accepted this as fact?

I am constantly *stunned* at how many men will not buy 'pons or pads on a trip to the store for fear of being embarrassed. Embarrassed by what? Are you worried that one of your friends might see you and think you were using them for yourself? A lot of guys try to overcome the fear by making a whole scene about it. "Yes, I am buying tampons today!"

What will it take to bring about a change? Does Walgreens need to hang enormous vinyl banners from the ceiling which read "WOMEN HAVE VAGINAS"?

I am always even more stunned at how many women are embarrassed to buy these products for themselves. Ladies, if you have your period, that's okay. You're SUPPOSED to have your period unless you're pregnant or menopausal. And let me assure you that when you become menopausal, if there is a 'pon/pad discussion going down the first thing you say is "I wish I still needed them," because I have heard this conversation like nine trillion times already.

Tampons cost roughly $5 for a box of just under 20. This year alone I have bought hundreds of boxes and been paid to take them. I don't really care if the sale is on chewing gum or maxi pads, it's all the same to me. The only thing was that in order to use the coupons to get the deal you really had to buy in multiples of 10.

So there I am shamelessly buying 40 or 50 boxes of 'pons in one transaction—big deal. And now just about every woman I know never has to buy them again for life. Plus, they were so happy at the women's shelter that we donated the rest of them to.

If you're a woman, how much does shame cost? Shame costs you $5 a month. Buy in bulk with no shame and get paid to take them next time. And there's never any reason to be shameful about your period. If the man you're with cannot cope with the fact that you're human, perhaps it's time to find someone else.

THE DIFFERENCE BETWEEN CHEAP & CHEAPSKATE

Speaking of your spouse not understanding, I know so many people whose spouses have been mortified when they have to go out in public with them after they have started coupon shopping. I never completely understand that because who wouldn't want to save money? But there is a line between being cheap and being an unbearable cheapskate.

Being cheap means you save money on things instead of wasting money on them. It means when you're alone you can inconvenience yourself to a degree in order to save a few bucks. It means you're practical about money.

Being an unbearable cheapskate means you probably need psychiatric help because your compulsion to avoid spending money may cause you or others physical pain or illness. For example, your daughter hurts her foot and instead of paying for a taxi to the hospital, you insist she take the bus because it's cheaper. Assuming, of course, that you have the money for a taxi and you're just refusing to spend it. As outrageous as that may sound, there are a *lot* of unbearable cheapskates out there. I've met my fair share.

When we drive two states away for pudding, it's an adventure, it's a sport, and in the end it's for charity. Hadn't we gone, we wouldn't be sitting at home with anxieties that someone else had gotten "our" pudding. Put in perspective, you know how to save money but you don't always *have* to save money.

WHEN TO QUIT

Another kind of shopper is the one who buys anything and everything just because it's on sale, having no need for the products themselves. We have all been guilty of doing this to some degree at one time or another, but it's another extreme to avoid. My experience is that most of these people binge-shop on things that are not particularly good values, but they tell you that they are.

The only time it's not a problem to buy things you don't need is when you're being paid to take them. This way you're earning some pocket money and getting things to donate to charity where they will hopefully be used by people who do need them; I try to fall into this category as much as possible. Shopping is a lot of work, and you can get paid for it if you try, and to be able to help others in the process is an excellent bonus.

THEY CALL ME "TERIYAKI SAM"

Doing this can blow up in your face sometimes. Kikkoman Teriyaki Sauce is the textbook example of how being paid to shop can cost you more money than you were paid. You might have to read that last sentence a few times because the irony is rather heavy.

Basically, the deal goes like this: buy two bottles of KTS; each one has a retail price of about $1.50, and when you ring them up at the register a coupon prints out for $3 off your next purchase of just about anything at the same store.

On the bottles themselves were coupons for 55 cents off each, which doubled, making each bottle roughly 40 cents each. So for 80 cents out of pocket, you were getting back a coupon for $3 off anything.

To translate, for every two bottles of KTS I bought, I was paid $2.20 profit. For those of you who don't understand how a coupon like this is profit, that's simple, it could be used to purchase postage stamps or even gift cards to use on things I would normally buy, like gasoline. You can also use a deal like this to take those coupons and stock up on things at the grocery store which never seem to go on sale. Perhaps you don't eat packaged food or use those kinds of products; you could then simply use the coupons to purchase produce or meats. You could use those coupons to buy diapers or formula. You could use those coupons for just about anything but lottery tickets because, first, there's probably a law and, second, because I would have to smack you upside the head for being so stupid.

You could further work the deal by buying multiple bottles in one order, and then paying for them with the $3 coupon as it printed out.

First order:

2 bottles – paid 80 cents – then received $3 coupon

Second order:

8 bottles - $3.20 total – pay with previous $3 coupon and 20 cents – then received $12 in coupons

Third order:

30 bottles - $12 total – pay with previous $12 in coupons – then received $45 in coupons

To be realistic, it would be hard to find a store that had more than 40 bottles in stock. Trust me on this one, I know. For each store you cleaned out, you would leave with $45, 40 bottles of KTS, and some very weird looks from the other customers, and all for just $1 out of pocket. You can imagine how many colors my face turns when I still see people paying $1.50 a bottle for the stuff.

This deal was so good that on several occasions we did not stop buying until the car was so packed with KTS that you couldn't see out the windows. It took over our dining room for a month. We would mockingly pose for photos outside the grocery stores with cartfuls of bottles, our teddy bear, and then tear out of the parking lots with the windows open, blaring "Cuyahoga" by R.E.M.

The entire ritual, like so many other things in my life, had become some sort of bizarre performance art with no audience. Whatever, it was fun and we got paid.

So what's that you say? What could be bad about a deal like this? Sounds like fun, right? Well, it's always fun and games until you have an apartment full of Teriyaki sauce that you discover is nearly impossible to give away. No wonder they were paying us to take it off their hands.

Kikkoman Teriyaki Sauce is a perfectly good product. We've obviously tried it by now, but we couldn't find anyone who used more than one or two bottles in a year. We spent weeks trying to pawn it off on anyone dumb enough to take it from us. Yes, we tried calling whatever kind of business you're thinking we should have called. Nobody wanted it.

Any friend we had who was stupid enough to leave their car running in front of our house had at least one case mysteriously appear in their trunk when they got home. The stories of how they tried to pawn it off were even better than the stories of how we got it. Food pantries were turning it away, and that's how you know it's useless.

While we could go back to the conversation about why they made it in the first place, let's leave that alone right now. Instead, let's talk about taking a deal too far. As in five or more states away too far.

AIRTRAN = VALUJET = CORPSES IN THE EVERGLADES

Earlier in the year Wendy's had a deal whereby if you cut coupons out of the soda cups, you could redeem them for free flights on Air Tran. I don't remember how many cups per flight it was, but I think it was around 50. Anyway, since we all know how much soda I drink, I had been checking out this guy on Craigslist who claimed to be selling the coupons in bulk. He wanted $25 per roundtrip ticket and you could have up to two round trips on each person's frequent flyer account.

We met at a fast food restaurant, where he walked around in circles shouting my name at everyone until he found me. Then he insisted on giving me a big hug before opening his backpack, which was full to capacity with the coupons cut out from soda cups. People inventing new industries love to brag about them and this guy was no exception. He had been hiring all the kids at school to hang out near the trash cans at Wendy's and take the soda cups off people's trays as they were throwing them out. In an afternoon, he had turned the sanitation industry on its ear. I nearly cried. It was so nice to see someone with real entrepreneurial spirit fighting back against the idiotic concept of paying $2 for a fountain soda.

When I got home, I filled out all the paperwork to send in the coupons and discovered most of them were still stuck together from the soda. I went ahead and sent the big mess off to Air Tran and a couple of weeks later, the miles were in our accounts.

So here we were up to our asses in Teriyaki sauce thinking about the greatest concentration of grocery chains participating in the promotion closest to an airport we could fly to on these tickets. One Saturday, in the course of about ten minutes, we packed up our car rental vouchers from another promotion and headed to Virginia—total airfare $19 each with taxes.

This began a nearly week-long drive home in which we stopped at every Food Lion, Weis, Shoppers Club, Ukrops, and anywhere else we could find to do the deal. We filled an entire SUV with KTS, until we encountered a new and completely unexpected problem.

Potential problems for most people might include reduced gas mileage, reduced visibility, and no room for luggage in the car, back and shoulder pain, mental disorder, or allergy to Teriyaki sauce. While these are all compelling arguments for avoiding such a journey, none of them bothered us. What did bother us was the start of a sale on Sunsilk shampoo and conditioner at CVS.

SILKY SMOOTH AND ON THE MOVE

Personally, I'd never heard of the stuff. I've been using Selsun Blue or Head & Shoulders for the better part of 20 years. The deal worked like this: they had trial size bottles on sale for $1.75 and for each one you bought I think they gave you $3 in "ExtraCare Bucks," which are essentially CVS gift certificates. The trial size bottles had coupons on them for $1 off, making them 75 cents. So for each trial size you purchased, you made about $2.25 profit.

This follows the same theme as the KTS, only you couldn't purchase gift cards or postage stamps this time.

There were larger bottles too, which were shipped to the stores in pre-packaged display cases; on those you paid $3, you used the same $1 off coupons, paid $2 out of pocket, and then got $3 ECB in return. So you made only $1 on the larger ones.

CVS's system works like this: let's say we buy four bottles of the shampoo, total cost $12. Now we give the cashier four coupons, each for $1 off; the subtotal is now $8. We pay the $8 and two days later, we receive a gift certificate for $12. Just like the KTS, we then use the $12 certificate to buy six bottles, no cash exchanges hands, and two days later we receive a gift certificate for $18. And so on and so forth.

ECB IN THE PLACE TO BE

To call this system perverse is an understatement. At this point CVS is literally printing money for us to use in order to buy more products, for which they are printing even more money for us to use to buy even more products, for which they are printing even more money for us to use to buy even more products, for which they are printing even more money for us to use to buy even more products, for which they are printing even more money for us to use to buy even more products, for which they are printing even more money for us to use to buy even more products, for which they are printing even more money for us to use to buy even more products, until we end up in a parking lot of a shopping mall in Delaware eyeing a giant fountain thinking about how to dispose of it all.

End result? We paid about $20 or so out of pocket and ended up with over $300 worth of CVS gift certificates and a car full of shampoo. You can use the gift certificates on things like OTC medication, Band-Aids, cleaning supplies, bread, milk, soup, and just about any other household staple you can think of. Even though CVS is overpriced, at a discount of over 90%, it's not too terrible. What may surprise you is that even with the 90% discount, some of the items were *still* overpriced. That was shocking enough to us!

Oh, and there's the small matter of the SUV full of free shampoo and teriyaki sauce.

When you get to that level of ECB use, you end up picking up the entire display of product and carrying it to the register. You also encounter a lot of resistance from the store employees and manager. The topic of whether CVS managers were lobotomized at birth is a popular topic on coupon shopping message boards, but let's discuss that a little later.

Just like in a casino, you end up having to toke the dealer, so when you buy a hundred shampoos, the cashier ends up with four or five. Sometimes if you're a regular at a store, you know all the cashiers' favorite candy bars, which you need for filler. Filler is when you have a coupon for $5 off an order of $20, but you only have $19 worth of merchandise, so you throw in a couple candy bars in order to use the coupon. "It costs less to spend more," another David Byrne photo exhibition idea. This one is perhaps black and white photographs of toasters or something?

We did manage to donate the majority of the shampoo and conditioner, but not before it literally filled the car to complete capacity. I drove past Food Lions and Weis stores hanging my head in shame that I could no longer buy more KTS. Somewhere around West Chester, Pennsylvania, it struck me that I could just buy bottles and leave them in the parking lot, so that's what we began to do. If you found a shopping cart full of KTS abandoned in a grocery store parking lot anywhere near the New Jersey Turnpike, that was me—you're welcome.

OPENING UP MY OWN METH LAB

Lest you think it was the first time I bought merchandise only to abandon it, let's talk cold medicine. We were on vacation and discovered a cold medicine deal in which we were making $2 a box on various brands of cold medicine. This was a trip where we had to fly home and so after the rental car was full we emptied the product into our hotel room, and repeated this over and over again during the course of a week.

Hours before getting on the plane we had to discuss what to do with a hotel room full of cold medicine, and we decided the best thing to do was simply leave it there. We could only imagine what the staff would think and, luckily for us, it was just weeks before the pseudoephedrine laws had been passed.

As I said before, sometimes the cashiers and store managers can be a real nightmare and when you walk up to a register wearing a Rolling Stones t-shirt, dancing to your iPod, taking photographs of a teddy bear, or you pull up in a rental car and try to buy a hundred boxes of cold medicine with a hundred coupons—well, you're just asking for trouble.

COUPON QUEENS ARE FULL OF IT

One of my favorite things is the "coupon queens" who go on TV and show you how they saved so much money by using coupons in bulk. It's a staple of local news shows all over the country and thanks to the Internet I get to see them all now. To anyone who does not know much about it they all seem impressive, but to those of us in the know, these queens are the subject of much ridicule. Go on any coupon message board the day after one of these things airs nationally and you'll get a clearer picture. How did she get $300 worth of groceries for $20? Well, usually she pads it up by using a lot of "Get one of our products free" coupons that you receive after you call a manufacturer's customer service number to complain/compliment a product. Those coupons can have a very high face value as a result, especially on things like cleaning supplies, so they kind of pad the sale. Another trick is to simply make it seem like you're getting a good deal. More recently, I've seen a lot of coupon queens on TV getting $300 worth of groceries for $200. Okay, so it's 30 percent off, but who cares? You should be working to save a minimum of 75 percent. Plus, if you're trying to send a message, at 30 percent off, chances are that someone is still making a profit, and what have you accomplished then? Consumer reporters on local stations are usually so full of themselves they don't really know what's a good deal and what's not, so long as they look like they are actively doing something about it.

This all brings us to the perfect example of a deal you never see a coupon queen do on television, but is the kind of deal that makes real coupon shoppers get out of bed at 5:00 a.m for days on end, and that deal was last known as "Crazy Eights."

ROLLING ROLLING ROLLING

The sale went like this: "Buy any eight products on this page, get $8 off your next order."

By now you're familiar with the system from the KTS deal, but what you may not be expecting is that some of the items were *also* on 10/10 that week. Frozen waffles, pancakes, and French Toast sticks were among them. Remember, on a 10/10 sale, you don't have to buy 10 items to get them for $1 each, you can just buy one. So we would go up to the register with 8 boxes of frozen waffles, pay $8, and then get a coupon for $8 off our next order, which, ironically, was another 8 boxes of waffles, which netted us another coupon to pay for another 8 boxes. With two full shopping carts and a "U-Scan" check-out, we cleaned out an entire store of all three varieties in a matter of minutes. Good thing we own a chest freezer; it was full to capacity, and we started pushing these things on the neighbors until their freezers were full as well.

Now look, you have to be really shameless and very demanding to insist that a store give you an entire freezer's worth of frozen waffles for a total of $8, but again, is $4.99 a box a fair price for that product? No, it's outrageous. Each box has 8 frozen waffles in it and probably costs less than 30 cents to manufacture.

Next up, Sunny Delight. I think it's a "Juice Flavored Drink," but I don't know; it's one of those mysteries of modern marketing. Anyway, the promotion was set up so that if you bought a few bottles, you got a couple of movie tickets with a mail-in-rebate. In the end, I think it worked out to two or three dollars per movie ticket while the drinks were on sale during the crazy eight promotions. In order to get the movie tickets, you had to remove the labels from the bottles and mail them in with the cash register receipt. The problem with Sunny Delight is it is loaded with sugar, the bottles are enormous, and we don't drink nearly enough of it to justify buying an entire shopping cart's worth. One bottle would probably last us six months, if not longer. So there I was in the parking lot with a shopping cart full of unlabeled bottles. Now you can't donate this stuff to the food pantries because they won't accept anything with the labels removed. You can't simply donate it to a school or give it to a homeless person because should anyone become ill from it (say, if a diabetic were to drink it without realizing the sugar content), you would be liable. I didn't want to drink it myself. I didn't even want to bring it home and have it take up room in our apartment. So what to do? You're standing around a parking lot with a shopping cart full of gallons of intentionally-screwed up drinking water in environmentally unfriendly plastic bottles. Listen, I would love to stand around all day and debate what to do with it but I didn't have time, because we still have crazy eights going on back in the store, so I simply abandoned it in the parking lot. Hopefully, nobody was going to call the cops thinking it was anything nefarious.

While crazy eights was still going on, there was another deal on the horizon—free soup. The free soup deal worked in a similar manner; the can of soup was on sale for $2. When you purchased one, a coupon printed out for $2.50 off "this OR your next order." The same week, canned vegetables were on sale for 50 cents. That's not really much of a sale; canned veggies should be more like 25 cents, but this was a "sale" according to the circular. So you brought the soup and veggies up to the cashier, who would ring them up, the $2.50 coupon would print right out, and then you could pay for them right then and there with the coupon making the product completely free. On my third trip up I figured it would take me all day to clean them out going one at a time, so I tried doing two at a time and indeed two of the $2.50 coupons printed out. Not being one to screw around when a good deal comes up, I then took a shopping cart and cleared out the entire shelf, along with a corresponding number of veggies. Sure enough, all 60 coupons printed out in one shot, and I was on my way.

Canned vegetables are never going to be in short supply around here, so

I was even more thrilled to discover the vegetable manufacturer had a mail-in-rebate going at the time, for which I received a rebate check for $15. So in the end, yes, I got paid to take 64 cans of soup and 64 cans of vegetables. When I see people paying $3 for a can of soup, it makes me want to beat them over the head with it. Of course, every once in a while I still pay $3 for a can of soup myself. Yes, it's true; I'm a sucker for Wegmans.

As for the Sunny Delight, this was not the first time I had gone nuts over a movie ticket promotion. A few weeks prior there had been one on breakfast cereal. This deal ended with me up standing in a parking lot handing out boxes of cereal like Santa Claus because the car was completely full. The movie tickets arrived in separate envelopes, piles of them at my front door. Now, it is true that I try to go to the movies every day, but these movie tickets were expiring soon. Here's a little known fact about movie tickets: they almost never expire. You go to the theater with your movie coupons from these promotions and you use them to buy tickets to any movie before they expire. The theater is reimbursed in full from the promotion house. Then take the tickets you receive at the theater and hold onto them. You can use them later simply by exchanging them for the movie, date, and time you choose. Unlike live event tickets, it is extremely rare to find movie tickets that say "no refunds, no exchanges." It should go without saying that you should redeem the initial movie certificates for evening performances, and not matinees, since you want the highest face value on the tickets you're redeeming them for.

THE WORLD'S DUMBEST PROMOTIONS

PART UN — UNIVERSAL ORLANDO MEETS THE ENTERTAINMENT BOOK

Marketing people always love to pat themselves on the back for great promotions, but I wish there were awards for the worst promotions, and perhaps the worst planned promotions as well. For example, a recent

Entertainment book had a coupon in it for simply "One free dinner and a movie pass" at Universal Studios Orlando. Now each pass would normally cost you $20, and by the end of the year an Entertainment book usually goes for less than $10, so the coupon itself is worth more than the book. I don't know who thought up this idea, but clearly they were rather swayed by Entertainment's own marketing.

Entertainment books are mostly used as fundraising devices by schools, churches, and other such organizations. They get the books at a substantial discount, with very little risk, and then sell them at good markups to the community, which receives an excellent value from them. It's a win/win situation. When you hear someone claim to be a bargain shopper or good with money and they tell you that the Entertainment book is not a good value, you know right then and there they have *no clue* what they are talking about and everything else they tell you is going to be total BS as well. So a lot of the people who sell these books end up with whole cases of them after the school year is over in June. Now the books are generally good until November 1st and because it is so expensive to ship back and for Entertainment to destroy, many salespeople end up just throwing the books away.

There are at least five different restaurants at Universal Citywalk for which you can use those coupons, and they include a complete meal, gratuity, and a movie ticket for any movie playing at the multiplex right there. Statistically speaking, there is at least one family in each of those schools who is going to Orlando for vacation that year. Had they asked the other parents for that coupon or gotten the remainder of the coupons from the salespeople at the school, they would have saved hundreds of dollars on food alone during their vacation. I understand most people wouldn't "waste time" going to the movies on their vacation, which is fine; they can give the tickets to me and I'll use them. Seriously though, can you imagine having access to all those free meal coupons and then going down there and spending money on the same exact meals? Statistically speaking, it happened tens of thousands of times last year. Well, I guess maybe the marketing people who came up with this one were not so stupid.

The coupons are redeemed for what look like admission tickets, which apparently don't expire for about 30 years, at which time (if the place is still standing) the free meal and movie tickets will hopefully seem like an even better value.

PART DEUX — PRIZE IN THE FOOD

In 1990, Coca-Cola introduced the "MagiCan," a "magic" can of cola, in which random cans filled with chemicals instead of soda would vend a rolled up piece of currency, such as a $10 or $50 bill when opened. The promotion was something of a disaster because many of the cans malfunctioned; in one case a plane was landed because the stewardess who opened it to serve to a passenger thought it might be an explosive device. Pepsi Cola had a similar promotion that year in which, if you had won money, a dollar amount would be printed inside the can at the bottom. There are no statistics as to how many people (who are now devout Coke drinkers) are walking around with one eye.

GE staged another poorly thought out promotion when it packaged random Target store gift cards in specially marked packages of lightbulbs. Since lightbulb packages are open on two sides, it was pretty simple to see which boxes had the gift cards in them and which didn't. On clearance at $2.48 a package, the customer realized an immediate profit of $2.52 (or more, since the cards were for random amounts, the lowest being $5) by in many cases simply removing the gift card from the package at checkout to pay for the lightbulbs up front. This meant the customer had to expend nothing in order to stock up on free lightbulbs and Target gift cards.

It was not long after that the great minds in marketing were back with another brilliant Target store item; this time it was clear plastic bags of candy corn, all of which had a gift card in them that was fully visible. The gift cards were worth nothing or $5. All you had to do was take the bags of candy to the in-store kiosks and use the "check gift card balance" feature in order to determine which of the 99-cent bags had $5 gift cards in them. At no time did you have to remotely damage the packaging or void any of the terms or conditions of the promotion. It was comical when you would walk in a Target and discover shopping carts piled high with bags of candy corn abandoned in front of the kiosks.

Yet my favorite was the Betty Crocker boxes of fruit snacks which randomly contained a $5 "BOOYAH" branded gift card. "Booyah" is of course urban slang for the noise a sawed-off shotgun makes when it is discharged. Within ten minutes of the boxes being shelved at a local grocery store, I witnessed children walking by and crumpling every box to determine which one had the gift cards inside and which didn't. Practically all of the remaining product on the shelf was then damaged to unsalable condition.

PART TROIX — SCAVENGER HUNT STYLE

Finding a good deal in a grocery store is often like a game of "Concentration": you have to remember where you saw something earlier and what it said. For a while, there were loaves of raisin bread made with a popular brand of raisins in them. As part of a cross-marketing effort, the loaves of bread had coupons on them for 50 cents off a box of the raisins, which doubled, and were normally priced at 99 cents. So walking into the store with no coupons, no plan, and no need to buy anything, it was easy to peel the coupons off the bread (these kinds of coupons called "peelies," are attached to the outside of a product with no cash value, meaning they are not part of the products packaging), and then redeem them all for a big shopping bag full of free raisins.

PART QUATRE — COUPON IN THE BOX

If you know what you're buying in advance, sometimes there are "hidden" coupons in a store; for example, the box of cookies that was on sale for $2 and when you ripped open the box, a coupon for $2 off was printed on the inside. The cookies were packaged in a plastic bag inside the box, so the cashier rang it up, you opened the box, ripped it apart, and then handed her the coupon right back to pay for them.

PART CINQ — PAY THE CUSTOMER OFF

There was a deal at one store where you bought a $4.99 sunscreen using a store coupon for $5, making it instantly free, and then you could submit a rebate online to get back another $2 per bottle with no limit.

PART SIX — BUY X NUMBER OF PRODUCTS – GET X AMOUNT OF MONEY

One of the best deals to look for is when you see a store advertising a rebate on their own private-label stuff. Usually stores issue $1 off any of their private-label products just as an incentive to get you to try them, since many people still don't believe in generics. Look for coupons like this along with a rebate, such as "buy any 10 of our private-label products and get a $7 rebate." Then what you do is simply find the cheapest private label product they make (it's often cough drops for 99 cents). So you buy 10 of the product, hand over 10 of the coupons (for a total price of -.10), then get a check in the mail for $7. You can throw out the cough drops or donate them to charity, because if you hang around us for more than five minutes you'll end up with a whole room of your house filled with them. I never feel the cough drops are strong enough so I end up buying the ones I like even though I have maybe 50 bags of generics sitting around the house. Who knows why exactly they make this stuff, but, like I keep saying, they are paying you to take them!

PART SEPT – FREE WORTHLESS ITEM WITH PURCHASE

Dominos Pizza ran a promotion in which if you ordered a pizza you could watch a trailer for the film *The Dark Knight* online after checkout. Apparently, no one at Dominos Pizza ever heard of YouTube, where the clip was copied and reposted almost immediately. And who the hell would order a pizza in order to watch a commercial? Someone who was stoned enough to order Dominos, I figure.

HOW STUPID DOES A MANUFACTURER THINK YOU ARE, EXACTLY?

Campbell's thought that their customers were having too much trouble opening a can of soup, so they began putting pop-tops on their cans, eliminating the need for a can opener. Okay, makes sense, I guess. Then they put a "Frequently Asked Questions" on their website with a list of can openers that were compatible with their new cans, the same ones, as I've said, that didn't require a can opener. To really confuse the shit out of you, they then sell a special tool that they invented to open their cans, the same ones which do not require a can opener. This is because they have not yet figured out how to sell you your own fingers, the ones needed to open their new cans which do not require the use of a can opener. Are you getting all of this?

Here's what I want to know. How frequently were they really asked, "How do you open these new cans?"

COUNTING SHEEP

A lot of people still do not know that you can use a manufacturer's coupon and a store coupon on the same item. Now remember, the terms and conditions of one of these coupons may specify that this is incorrect, but a majority of the time it is. This can lead to really great deals that never would appear in a circular.

The best is when you find a coupon for an item to make it free sitting right next to the item itself. One time we found an entire tearpad of 75¢ off one item from an organic brand. Organic Mac & Cheese was $1.50 and the coupon doubled. Another time, and this was one of my favorites, chocolate milk was on sale for $1 and directly above them was a "blinkie" machine (one of the machine that spits out one coupon at a time every few seconds) loaded to the gills with $1 off coupons. I actually took a lawn chair from seasonal and dragged it to the milk case to sit and watch people buy chocolate milk for an hour, and not ONE took the coupon directly above it which would make it free.

As an experiment, I took a few of the coupons and stood there offering them to people as they took the milk off the shelves. Each time I explained how the milk was free with the coupon. A couple of people said "thank you," and scurried away. The rest treated me like I was an evil marketing person handing out advertising for something they didn't need or want, like the product they had chosen and was in their hand. Some thought I was surely trying to get them involved in some kind of scam. It was a very interesting afternoon.

I am fascinated by the fact that Nigerians can bilk Americans out of their life savings with a couple of emails and phone calls, but it's nearly impossible to stand in a public place in America and give away free money. Is it any wonder the Nigerians are so proud to be scamming money from us that they have hit records and music videos all about it?

ALL ROADS POINT TO WAWA

We visited a store once (named Wawa) that had coupons printed on the back of the ATM receipts. So I took the entire trash bag full of ATM receipts over to the coffee bar and sorted them out on the table. There was some interesting stuff, but nothing I actually needed or could use on that trip. Who knows, perhaps you may find something in there without having to go through the whole bag. My point is you need to look everywhere because the coupons are hiding in the strangest places, like directly above the merchandise, for example.

Wawa is practically a religious institution in some parts of the country, but most people understand it just to be a convenience store. On the refrigerators at a Wawa in Pennsylvania, we spotted some coupons for 75¢ off any one Snapple, which was going for about $2 at Wawa. We knew they generally cost about $1 everywhere else, so we took the entire pad of coupons down the street to Genuardis, who advertised in big letters on the window, "Unlimited Double Coupons," meaning if we had, say, 83 Snapple coupons for 75¢ each, they would double all of them in one order (most stores impose a limit as to how many of the same coupon they will double in an order). So, if we were to, say bring 83 bottles of Snapple to the register with 83 coupons, they would all be free, and they nearly were! We had to pay tax on the ones that were not iced tea (they don't tax tea in Pennsylvania). The total was somewhere under a dollar for a car trunk full. Good value.

MEET THE COUPON FAIRY (HE'S A BREEDER)

Security cameras have often captured me accosting other customers who I see paying full price for things. Sometimes I "coupon fairy" people who are buying products for which I have a coupon that would get them the item for free. Half the people say thank you and are appreciative, and the other half have no idea what I'm giving them, like I am handing out flyers for a band or something.

What I have learned is some people really *enjoy* overpaying for things. Some people feel it is a badge of honor. "Do you know how much I paid for this?" "Do you know what that costs?" "Do you know what that's worth?"

THAT ONE THING

Those people have something else in common; each has one secret item that they do not like to pay for. I do not know why that is—perhaps it was a traumatic allowance deficiency in their youth—but each has one item that makes them almost angry to pay for. The usual culprits are razors, batteries, cat litter, Costco memberships, and Starbuck's coffees.

To make you look smart around them, let's play with that for a minute.

THE CUTTING EDGE

Razors – a bit tricky but not impossible. One of the great things about doing razor deals is you always get the newest, latest, greatest razor out there. That is pretty much the key to the whole thing. Gillette and Schick are both constantly coming out with new styles of razors and when they launch each one there are great promotional campaigns. These campaigns usually involve high value coupons in the Sunday paper, which you can combine with "free-after-rebate" deals at the major drug chains in order to get paid to take the razors. But what do you do after the initial campaign is over? No sweat. One of the most popular razor coupons is "buy a refill, get a free handle." Great news, one of the most popular razor sales is "buy a handle, get a free pack of refills." All you do is look for a week when you have that coupon and a store is running that sale, present the coupon and get both for free.

Let me slow it down for you.

Store says buy a handle, get free refills

Manufacturer says buy refills, get a free handle

Translation:

Store says if you buy a handle, we pay for your refills

Manufacturer says if you buy refills, we pay for your handle

And if you search hard enough I'm sure there's a video out there of me wearing a crooked baseball cap and standing at a Rite Aid while counting out 50 razor coupons like they were ill-gotten funds, a stack of razors on the counter in front of me, saying "MO MONEY MO MONEY MO MONEY!"

People act crazy when you give them $500 worth of razors for free, especially those who like to brag about how much they pay for stuff.

MORE POWER TO YOU

Batteries – another popular favorite. Some places you can still do the old-style battery deals, which were the same as deodorant: $1 off coupon, to use when they would go on sale 10 for 10. At that time, they still sold a lot of 2-packs of batteries. When we started doing coupon shopping seriously, I had a lot of trouble finding any stores that still sold AA or AAA batteries in packages of 2. They are impossible to find in almost any chain store. This probably has to do with the fact they were nearly $4 a pack before they were discontinued. Now that there are so many new types of batteries, some costing as much as $4 or $5 per battery, the whole nature of battery deals has changed. That's okay; we can still get them for free with a little work.

First off, let's talk about those "ultra alkaline," "extra pure digital" batteries and the like. These are the batteries which have so much packaging you would think they could be used to impregnate someone from outer space and should be kept in a super-freezer under tight security. As I said before, each battery has a retail price of about $4 each. Do they really keep your iPod or cellphone running longer? No, of course not, both have rechargeable batteries. You can assume that anyone stupid enough to pay $4 for one AA battery is going to believe that their Discman will spin for weeks on one of these, and I pray that this is true because the longer we keep those people off the streets, the better.

Each of those brands of batteries has a satisfaction guarantee mail-in-rebate usually right on the front of the package, and high value coupons because of the outrageous price. So if a pack of four is $16, you can find a $4 off coupon in the paper, pay $12, then mail in the receipt, UPC, and a 3x5 index card explaining why you didn't like the product, and get a rebate of the original $16 price, so the $4 profit more than covers your postage. You can only do one per brand, which is fine because there seems to be another new brand every time you go back to the store for new ones. You have not lived until you have found a legitimate reason to send Energizer a note which reads, "Batteries died in my vibrator mid-course, and I had to finish myself manually." Obviously, nobody is reading the 3x5 index cards, but they request you put them in there anyway, so, as they say at the sandwich shop, "Be Creative!"

Second, many of the dollar chains now sell four packs of batteries for $1 but they do not accept manufacturer's coupons. I have sent letters in the past asking about this and they usually send back rote replies that say something along the lines of "We do not accept coupons, as our prices are so low already, they are not necessary for you to use!"

I usually tell the letter to kiss my ass before throwing it in the ever-increasing "Show Research" folder.

So the new battery deals go like this: really large packages of batteries, 12 or more, will now go on sale at the grocery chains for $2 or so. The coupons in the paper are usually still for just $1 off on these kinds of batteries. You end up paying $1 for 12, not free, but if you have to pay for them it's still a tremendous savings over the $5 or more everyone else has to pay for them.

REPORTS OF A LOUD ODOR ABOUND

Cat litter is another 10 for 10 item with a $1 off coupon. The problem here is that there are lots of crazy people who live alone with 30 cats and no income. Every time cat litter goes on sale like this the shelves are bare within 20 minutes of the store opening. No sweat. Go to the customer service desk and get a "raincheck." A raincheck is a voucher which says that when the item is back in stock you can purchase it at the sale price, even if the sale is over. Yes, you can use your coupons with the raincheck as long as the coupons have not expired.

A little bit of work is required here. You have to remember to go back to the store before the next cat litter sale and after the shelves have been restocked, usually a month after the sale is over, but when you do it is easy to clean them out. You still have to pay tax since cat litter is not food, but paying under $3 for 300 lbs. of cat litter will not only break your back, damage your car, get you some interesting looks, but, most importantly, it will make your cat really happy, and what else matters? Of course, many people feel that this is too much work and would rather buy cat litter in bulk at a Costco or Sam's Club.

WHOREHOUSE CLUBS

Costco memberships have gotten out of control. $50 a year? They are on drugs. Even worse, if you go on their website, on the same page that casually informs you that the membership now costs $50, they brag about how much money they made last year. This deal works at all three warehouse clubs—

Costco, Sam's, and BJ's. Each of these clubs has a no-questions-asked, non-expiring refund policy. You just need to remember to cancel every 364 days, which, if you have a calendar and plan accordingly, is very easy to do. As long as you get a refund within 364 days, you can sign up again on your next visit and cancel again the following year. If you're really lazy, just let your membership lapse after a few months and each generally sends a coupon for a discount if you rejoin.

Some of you are reading that considering it to be dishonest or worse. No, it is not. It is pure capitalism. It's one of those deals people look at and think it's shady or they feel uncomfortable with it. That's what I was talking about earlier— how you pay avoid feeling shame.

How do you justify charging $50 a year for people to have the *permission* to *shop* at your *store*?? The whole membership club pricing routine is a big mind game and nothing else. If you gave $50 to the church, cancer research or to the Girl Scouts then okay, you should be polite and not expect anything in return. This is a *retail store* in business to *make money*. If you give them $50 you had better get something for it. All you essentially get is *permission* to *shop* in *their store*. Technically, membership includes approximately fourteen additional benefits, most of which are intended for business members (such as credit card processing), but let's take a quick look at the nine which are intended for individuals or families. Two are related to purchasing and financing an automobile, which in the current economic climate are easy to find a discount on. One is for a high-yield savings account which is comparable to Emigrant Direct or ING Direct, neither of which require a membership fee. There are two related to buying and selling a home, services which you can't spit without finding someone willing to offer you those services at cut-rate prices. One offer is for Sharebuilder.com, a website which offers all sorts of promotions, again, without the purchase of an external membership required to take advantage of. The final offer is for the printing of personal checks, with the comical notation that you can save up to 50% "compared to bank pricing," which is notoriously high. In any Sunday paper you can get checks printed by a third-party advertiser for ten dollars or less. This brings me back to the idea that the main benefit, essentially the only real benefit to membership, is the permission to shop in the store. Here's what the Costco membership benefits brochure fails to mention: if you shop at Costco and pay with a Costco gift card you don't need to be a member. Sure, you have to be a member to purchase the gift cards, but you don't need to be a member in order to redeem them.

It is debatable whether the store even offers any bargains that you will take advantage of, as a great deal of the merchandise is overpriced. If you can get razors for free at CVS with coupons, paying $20 for them in any quantity is no longer a value.

Warehouse clubs are reasonable in the fact that they offer these refunds because even they know it's a bit outrageous to expect that people will pay for the permission to shop in their store, but barely anyone takes them up on it for fear of being embarrassed or at worst inconvenienced. That's practically a protection racket. "If you pay us $50, you won't have to wait in line at our customer service desk to get it back."

The whole routine is such a farce; the back story is that once you pay to join a warehouse club you have pooled your money with all the other members to cover the operating costs so you can all purchase merchandise at a price very close to wholesale. Come on, in my view, it hasn't been that way in a very long time. If you want that, go join a food co-op or a barter group of some sort. I am sure Costco, BJ's, and Sam's Club all realize a very healthy profit on the merchandise sold or they wouldn't be opening in every shopping center in the country.

You should not be embarrassed, concerned, shamed, or feel that it is "wrong" to cancel your membership and get a refund. If they ask you why you're canceling, it's simple: the fee is too high and you would rather keep your money than give it to them when they certainly don't need it and provide absolutely nothing in return for it.

When one of the largest retailers in the country demands almost half a week's paycheck for someone on minimum wage for the permission to shop in their store in the guise of saving that person money down the road, do you really need to help them further their cause?

Hell, for $50 a year they don't even give you shopping bags. I mean, it's like some kind of sick joke. "How little can we give the consumer and how much can we get them to pay for it?"

Generally, I like to put the $50 on whichever 0% interest/no annual fee credit card I am rocking that year. Some bank can loan them the $50 for free, so why should it come out of my pocket?

The worst misconception I have ever seen applied to the perceived savings was that of a politician, Councilman Eric Gioia of New York who publicly urged Costco to accept public assistance (food stamps in New York are distributed on credit-card-style cards known as EBT or Electronic Benefit Transfer) EBT cards for payment so that the people on food stamps who needed to stretch their dollars further could take advantage of the savings. It was a completely outrageous suggestion and when I called his office to explain to him why I felt it was outrageous, he didn't meet with me but instead sent two young assistants who had no clue what I was talking about. Neither one had ever so much as clipped a coupon in their lives. While I am supportive of the food stamp program, it continues to astound me how few people use coupons in conjunction with their food stamps and the sorts of products, such as soda and cookies, which may be paid for with food stamps. Every time I have offered to teach food stamp recipients how to use coupons for free out of the goodness of my heart I have been turned down.

From my perspective, it seems as if the food stamp program is a bit of a sham intended to get uneducated consumers to spend top dollar for center-store packaged goods and then have the taxpayers pay for it. Why there isn't any sort of mandatory class on basic money management and saving money required before public assistance is granted to a recipient I don't know. Again, let me be clear, I am not for discontinuing the programs, shrinking the programs, making it harder to receive assistance, or anything similar. I am only suggesting that the programs be made as beneficial to as many people as possible, so that as a taxpayer I can be assured my money is doing the most amount of good for the largest number of people. As it stands now, the only people I see truly benefiting from public assistance are the packaged goods manufacturers and the retailers.

DON'T GET BURNED
(THESE JOKES ARE GETTING WORSE)

Starbucks is a place we all know is a terrible value but we go there anyway. I've already talked about that, but how to save money there is a bit of work. The good thing about the popularity of Starbucks is how many companies use their gift cards as premiums. Starbucks basically only runs one major promotion from time to time. When you register a Starbucks Gift Card on their website and link it to your credit card, after you load $20 on it they will add $10 free. After you get the $10, they expect you will keep your credit card set up to auto-renew, keeping them flush with your money, and ensuring that you mindlessly pay with the gift card for eternity. Of course, all you have to do is cancel the subscription online as soon as you get your $10, which most people forget to do. Starbucks is not so much a coffee company as they are a financial services company that specializes in a legal form of milling, but then again Boston Market is a real estate company that just happens to sell chicken dinners. Seriously, I love America.

SUNDAY EVENING

Let me clue you in to what coupon shoppers are doing on Sunday nights; we are gearing up to go get all the unsold Sunday newspapers. Usually we start around 11 p.m. Before the garbage trucks have started in our area, all the stores that sell newspapers have neatly bundled their unsold papers and placed them outside next to the trash, so pull up to each one and throw the bundles in the trunk. Just like our other pursuits, we don't stop until the car is so full that you can't see out of the windows.

Shattering to your vision of cuddling near the fire with a cup of hot chocolate though it may be, for bargain hunters it's just as romantic and exciting.

A lot of our friends who live in more suburban places wait until Monday or Tuesday when they can stop by the local recycling center and go through all the discarded papers in order to remove the coupon books.

Once we get home, we hang out in the driveway for a couple of hours separating the coupons from the rest of the papers and then putting the papers in recycling bags. Sometime after that Jean usually goes to sleep and I stay up in the kitchen listening to music and cutting up all the coupons into a big pile.

For the next couple of nights we spend a few hours sorting all those coupons into our binders and boxes so that we can find them easily when there is a sale. Yes, it's a lot of work, but for the maybe five hours work we generally save upwards of a thousand bucks, so it is time well spent. Besides, we crack jokes and listen to the radio, which is a lot nicer than a lot of the dates my friends tell me they've gone on.

WHEN GARBAGE BAGS GO 10/10, WE GO APESHIT

Sometimes we get an idea in our heads and won't let it go, like the time we were working on a garbage bag deal. Now garbage bags are one of those items that before we were coupon shopping always caused us great anguish. Fifty bags retailed for somewhere between $5 to $8, and it just felt like we were getting mugged every time we had to buy a box. There was a coupon out for $1 off any size, and Stop & Shop was selling something weird like a 12-count box for $1. The morning the sale started, we were able to grab a few boxes locally, but we kept coming up empty-handed at our standby Stop & Shop. A couple of days passed and even though we already had an entire closet filled with free garbage bags from another promotion, it was just one of those deals we both felt we had to get in on. Perhaps it was because we felt we had finally outsmarted the evil garbage bag empire that had imprisoned us in the past or perhaps we were just bored, I don't know. So we hopped in the car, turned up the radio, and proceeded to drive up a good portion of the Boston Post Road (a local road that runs from New York to Boston), stopping at every single Stop & Shop along the way. What really made an impression on us was not the fact that we were nuts enough not only to do something like this on a Saturday night when most of our friends were getting drunk and going to nightclubs, but that we came up empty at every single Stop & Shop along the way.

In the end, we had gotten more trash bags at our local Stop & Shop to begin with than we did on the whole evening's drive. Of course, we got lots of rainchecks, and eventually used them all to corner the market on free trash bags, but it was interesting to consider. Had everyone else known about the trash bag deal? Did Stop & Shop simply not have the products in stock to begin with? Was there some great conspiracy here waiting for Mel Gibson to try to explain? I don't know; all I do know is we could have saved $30 in gas sitting at home getting rainchecks locally.

SORTING Q'S
(THAT'S SLANG FOR COUPON)

Complicated systems for coupon shopping abound. Buying expensive sorting boxes and books, making labels of such minutiae that it takes a small team of lawyers to decide which folder each coupon should go in, walking around the store holding 30 different-colored envelopes until you have a seizure over by the Pop Tarts and they have to call an ambulance. While in the past I have tried most of these systems in an attempt to find one that really worked, I have moved on to my new "don't plan" system.

My new "don't plan" system works like this; we have two boxes of coupons in the car, one for food items, and one for non-food items. When we get to a grocery store, I don't even bring the coupons in; first, I sit down and read the store ad at the store. No need to feel like a third-grader preparing for a math quiz. Either I read the circular at the coffee bar or on the toilet. Sometimes I start on the toilet and end up at the coffee bar or vice versa. It can take me a while to read the whole thing.

READ EV'RY PACKAGE,
CLIMB EV'RY MOUNTAIN,
'BREVIATE EVERY OTHER WORD

For a second, let's stop and talk about that— how long it takes to read a grocery store advertisement properly. Have you ever looked at the items in a grocery store? This is a very good exercise and if you have never done it I really want you to go out and try it. I think you may find it will really alter your perspective on everything to do with the food supply in our country today. Go to a store that sells groceries, then pick any aisle, find just one type of item, like cookies, and then one at a time, slowly read each and every package on the shelf as if it were some sort of instruction manual. If there is anything on the package (other than an ingredient) that you have never heard of and don't understand be sure to stop and take the time to find out what it means. This exercise will take about an hour, maybe an hour and a half. You will learn that all sorts of things now exist that you had no idea existed before. It truly is a wonder of modern marketing how much we filter out. Sometimes you need to put on some headphones and listen to music to filter out the loudspeaker advertising in the store, but with a little concentration you can do this exercise and you will be completely overwhelmed when it is over. Not just at the selection of the cookies, but as you walk out of the store you'll realize it is just one small portion of the offerings in this entire room, well, what more can I say? You need to just try it for yourself.

With that in mind, let's get back to my story about how to find some deals.

BACK TO SORTING Q'S

After I have read the entire circular, then I begin to piece together offers like a puzzle. My favorite thing is when the stores have store coupons printed right in the ad, that's much easier for me to work with. Often, I don't even have to go out to the car, such as one time when the coupon was good for 35 cents off any generic product. The coupon didn't say "Limit One Per Customer."

Let me tell you how much fun a coupon like that can be, and if you have children who are old enough that you feel comfortable letting them run around a store on their own, not only can you make grocery shopping really fun for them with a coupon like this, but you can save a ton of money.

So I had 35 cents off any store-brand generic product. I put on "Black & Blue" by the Rolling Stones (since this store brand logo was in black and blue), and I slowly walked each and every aisle twice (once on each side) carefully looking for the most inexpensive store-brand item I could find. Sure, there is something wrong with a grown man clapping his hands and singing "Hot Stuff" as he cruises down grocery store aisles in a solitary game of scavenger hunt, but I'm not hurting anyone and I'm actually being more productive and useful to society (since you know whatever we score is going to end up at charity) as a customer in that location at that moment than anyone else in there.

I found what I was looking for in aisle fourteen—baking. Hero (our manager) loves that aisle. Corn muffin mix was on sale this week for — wait for it— 35 cents a box. How many coupons did I have? As many as I wanted, all I had to do was keep ripping them out of the circulars piled a mile high at the front door. By the time we got to "Crazy Mama," I had a full shopping cart with around 70 boxes and a pocketful of the coupons ready to go at checkout.

After I put the boxes in the trunk, most people would have been very excited to get $24.50 worth of anything for free; those people are a little something I like to call "amateurs." Like a true consumer, I popped into the coffee bar, got a fresh cup, threw on "Metamorphosis" and headed back to aisle fourteen to get back to work. I struck gold again on boxes of matches, but we didn't really need them, and sometimes you just think about having your trunk full of a certain item and you say to yourself "bad idea," and leave it at that.

I use a similar system when buying other things using a lot of coupons. Those of you who are coupon shoppers already may get anxious or nervous when approaching a checkout with 40 or more coupons— worried about how the cashier will treat you or maybe worried that you got all the math right. So many times when you're off on your count you end up paying full price for an extra item and most of you say you were too nervous to catch it, and besides, what's an extra $5 when you've gotten 200 for free?

Calm down there, Jumpy. Coupon shopping is supposed to be a fun, relaxed, enjoyable sport or hobby. If you like making yourself crazy, go lock yourself in a room with three retarded adults who don't speak your language on unicycles and a box of razor blades; don't start making everyone else nuts at the grocery store just because you can't figure out where your paycheck went. We've already established where most of it has probably gone.

HOW TO ARGUE WITH A CASHIER

Imagine you're in a court of law. You do not have or need a lawyer in this court and best of all, there is nothing at stake. The entire burden of proof is on the cashier, not you. So when there is any kind of dispute, don't think twice, it is always going to be the cashier's fault. Yes, the cashier will always call a head cashier when there is a dispute and, guess what, it's the head cashier's problem as well. Many times the head cashier just shakes their head "no" at a coupon and walks away; that's when I get good and flip out on them for not having any manners.

In the meantime, let me just drive the message home that when you approach a cash register with 35 items and 35 coupons, you should feel perfectly calm; everything should be business as usual and you should feel happy that you're leaving with a shopping cart full of free merchandise. That's why you do this, to get free stuff, to feel good about it, and to help others. Arguing with cashiers goes with the territory, but once they identify you as "a screamer," they tend not to argue with you again in the future. If it weren't illegal, I'd have no problem simply taking a leak on their counter and barking like a dog. Anything to shut them up and let them keep their personal drama to themselves and not take it out on you; it's not your fault they're actually working in a grocery store and paying full price for groceries, all for much less than what you can get paid to pour soda down the drain.

Don't think I haven't read my fair share of complaint letters from cashiers who listen to our radio show, angered at not only being called "stupid," but because we're for encouraging consumers to stick up for themselves at the cash register.

My reply is always the same. If you're a good cashier and you understand how to read the terms and conditions on the coupons, you should have basically no disputes with any customer who is legally and legitimately trying to redeem coupons at your register. A good cashier knows how coupons work just as well as the consumer does and so there wouldn't be any need for any altercation. So if you're a good cashier, you shouldn't encounter any hostility from legitimate coupon shoppers. No, obviously I am not talking about people trying to scam you and I am not encouraging anyone to scam you. Therefore, the people I am talking to, the people I am encouraging to coupon shop, should cause you absolutely no problems whatsoever and hopefully will even tip you with one or more of the free items they receive.

But a good cashier such as yourself surely must know exactly how stupid the good majority of your coworkers seem to be.

Why does it always take three people to ring up any store coupon, which has explicit step-by-step instructions for the cashier printed at the bottom about how to ring it up?

While corporate culture would dictate that management is at fault in this particular instance, I would say a basic lack of common sense and possibly illiteracy is at fault. True, management is to blame for hiring people with a basic lack of common sense who are possibly illiterate, but if you had half a brain after working in a grocery store for a year, you'd be abandoning hotel rooms full of cold medicine instead of working on your feet in eight-hour shifts.

I get a lot of complaint letters from cashiers telling me that coupons won't help them get out of the financial situation they're in, to which my stock reply is simple. If you use coupons properly on all the items you normally buy in the course of a year, it's not hard to save $3000 in a year. You can then take that $3000 and use it towards something to help get you out of the situation you've found yourself in. It's a very basic answer with a basic message, but often you don't have to look past the fake designer sunglasses, shirts, pocketbooks, and shoes to tell why the cashier is having trouble making ends meet. Let's not forget the cellphones they have trouble staying off of or the instant lottery tickets they cannot stop scratching.

To me, this turns places like shopping malls into consumer playgrounds. When you can pit the stores against each other, when you can find a coupon at one and use it at another, when you have the ability to manipulate the price you pay completely legally and within the various store policies set forth by the stores themselves, then you, the consumer, can tell the gum-chewing, cellphone-talking, "Versache"-sunglasses-wearing snot of a cashier to go screw themselves whenever they say something you don't like. The nihilistic and almost dictatorial manner in which corporations try to determine how you "will" and "want" and "need" to buy things and at a price that only exists because you, the consumer, let it exist. I'm sure plenty of market research firms have also seen people pay for chocolate milk and so they figure why charge $1 when we can easily bilk these people for $2? Meanwhile I'm standing there trying to give chocolate milk away and I would have had better luck asking each stranger to perform a sex act on me right then and there.

HEY, NORM!

Watching people behave the way they do in the grocery store is about a billion times better than going to a zoo to look at caged animals. Caged animals are creatures of habit, but humans in the grocery store are as unnatural and insane as any creature on the planet. When I go to a grocery store (or anywhere else, for that matter) I behave the way most people would behave in a bar. I socialize with everyone; I like to hang out, talk it up, play dumb games, have a snack and something to drink, and then roll on home. For me, the place is about social interaction as much as it is the products being sold. We have no town square or main streets left; shopping malls had replaced them for a while, but no longer. The human spirit, the human need for the existence of community, has been marginalized to a few aisles surrounded by packaged edible items (should we really call half the shit in a grocery store "food"?)

This is completely alarming to the other customers and the staff. People are so disconnected from reality when they walk into one of these stores, which are designed to look almost like stage sets, that when a stranger approaches them and wants to have a conversation they either expect that you want something from them or that you want to harm them. Initiating any kind of casual conversation with any stranger in a grocery store is sure to get you a lot of strange looks and strange responses. What kind of bizarre world are we living in that people who don't know each other aren't even supposed to talk to each other? How are we expected to communicate as human beings? Behind a veil of privacy in Internet chat rooms and message boards? It doesn't make any sense.

As for the retailers, one of the best ways to generate repeat business is by engaging your customers. Once a week for eight years, I have ordered a pizza from the same pizzeria, owned by the same three guys the whole time. Yet every time I call, they don't recognize my voice, they don't remember my address, and I have to give them the whole order from scratch. At one point, about six years ago, I made a point to go in to the shop, introduce myself, learn their names, so hopefully I could just call them up and say, "Hey Tom, it's Sam, can you send over the usual?" But alas, they couldn't have cared less. I still order from them (because they do have great pizza), but the lack of engagement is pathetic. Why do people feel that only in the past should a store employee remember your name and your purchasing habits? I know a lot of employees' names, but that's because they've offered me such horrendous service that I've had to learn them in order to send in complaint letters about them. None of them knows mine.

The ultimate in disconnect is at Wal-Mart or Target, where the store does not even offer a frequent shopper card to analyze your purchases; they only focus on what products have been sold in what quantity and at what times. The customer's name (or personality) is completely irrelevant.

More than ever social interaction is key to an enjoyable experience at a grocery store, which is why it's so depressing to buy food at places like Wal-Mart, where it is nearly impossible to socialize when you're looking at hundreds of the most depressed people you have ever seen cruising the aisles and buying overpriced goods because they feel it's the "only place they can afford to buy these things." The truly weird thing about the whole culture is that the shopping carts at Wal-Mart are packed to capacity, while in wealthy neighborhoods the carts are empty. This would seem to go completely against the stereotypes perpetrated by television commercials and other forms of marketing. People will stampede a Wal-Mart and buy everything on the shelves, leaving trails of merchandise on the floor, but someone might go to Nordstroms and shop for hours without ever purchasing anything at all. Whenever I visit a Wal-Mart, I look for anyone wearing a suit. If you can find anyone wearing a suit, follow them around and watch them; it's better than watching a caged animal at a zoo perform any kind of unique ritual.

LET'S GO SCARE THE SUITS

Just like the looks of the faces on the animals at the zoo, people have different mannerisms when they go grocery shopping. On our trip up the Boston Post Road, I discovered how in really wealthy parts of Connecticut people are ashamed to be seen buying groceries, although I have yet to completely understand why. They look like sixteen-year-old boys trying to buy condoms. First they pretend not to be looking at the box of rice. They put on a big show of scanning the whole rice area. Perhaps they pick up a different box than the one they want and give a nod. "Hmmm," they say to the invisible man who is watching them and might accuse them of buying rice. Another look to see if the coast is clear before selecting the box they actually want and then sort of tossing it in the cart while looking the other way so they can claim it was an accident if questioned. Should you say, "hey, that rice is great!" they look like a deer in headlights and then they scatter away quickly and quietly. They'll come back to the store later and try again.

What's especially sad in these wealthy areas is you know these are the same people making the decisions about what is to be sold and how much the asking price should be. I often like to engage in my own version of class warfare by pretending to be a loud-mouthed redneck and chasing people through the store and saying things that I know will mortify them. "WHY-DYA THINKA THESE HERE TAMPONS?" I'll ask a pink-sweater-wearing housewife with a string of pearls around her neck and a multi-millionaire executive husband at home who is probably on the board of directors of a Fortune 500 company. "MY WIFE CALLS THESE ONES 'THE SHREDDERS' CAUSE THEY CUT HER UP, KNOW WHAT I MEAN?" I keep trying to make one of them faint and I'm sure with just a little more practice sooner or later I will meet and exceed my goal. My act is so uncanny that if you had seen it in person you would never believe that I was the same person who wrote this book. Any time you encounter some service being provided in an overly pretentious manner, please consider it your duty to do your very best "Larry the Cable Guy" impression. I once had a tailgate party in the lobby of a Four Seasons while wearing a Jeff Gordon t-shirt. It is important for those who feel superior to know that anyone with a few dollars in their pocket is able to bring their whole imaginary world crashing down with a flick of the wrist (I flicked open a can of Natural Ice, which I referred to as "a can of whoop-ass"). For the record, I know the address of almost every major art gallery in Manhattan by heart.

Why must we mock pretentious behavior? Because in a setting like this manners are considered a sign of respect and generally, I have very little respect for the people who would stay in a $600 per night hotel. The people who aspire to that kind of lifestyle are mostly corporate executives. Perhaps once upon a time this was a lifestyle to admire, but the world has clearly changed. With a corporate culture openly geared toward selling people things they don't need at prices they cannot afford, these are not people you can have very much respect for.

At a conference recently I heard someone from Kroger Supermarkets quote Nelson Mandela and relate it back to their own work. It is this same mindset that has spread like a disease through our culture and has fostered the production of faux-luxury products like Pringles Select, M&M Premium, and Folgers Gourmet. I know it's hard for most of these people to believe, but selling packaged foodstuffs is not akin to fighting apartheid.

By now you probably think I am generalizing and coming up with more conspiracy theories, but head on down to the library and pull out any of the books by Paul Mazur, a banker at Lehman Brothers who published bestselling manifestos beginning in the 1920s, in which he dictates that in order for our economy to survive we must use propaganda to convince ordinary citizens that they are to consume as many goods as possible, regardless of need. Beginning in the 1930s, the National Association of Manufacturers (the largest lobbying organization in the United States) then hired Edward Bernays to begin a public relations campaign essentially to promote this initiative.

Who was Edward Bernays? He was Sigmund Freud's nephew, the man who coined the term "public relations." Shortly before his death in 1995, he freely admitted that it meant nothing more than "propaganda," but because the Nazis had made "propaganda" sound like a "bad word" to the American public, he just called it "public relations."

In the Library of Congress you may find many of Bernays' papers in which he boasts about his success in doing things like getting women to smoke by making them feel it was a sign of rebellion (his client was cigarette manufacturers). These basic propaganda tactics are still used to this day and they are still used by many of the same lobbying groups that were initially using them in the 1930s. It is sickening that huge numbers of the people employed by these very companies as "executives" (even the word itself sounds like it has stature) are clueless as to how this form of class warfare (consumerism) is working and why it is working (propaganda).

To get yourself good and infuriated at the entire system, just go to a trade show. Pick one, any one, in just about any industry— it doesn't have to be food-related. Look at all the waste, listen to the people, and watch what they do. Recently I attended a grocery-related one and listened to a man with no talent, no life skills, and no common sense yell into his cellphone that "they" had booked him in the wrong hotel because his hotel didn't serve some specific kind of meal, which is his favorite. "I don't like [the other one]!" He insisted. "Do you want me to move product or not? Then I have to be comfortable!"

After you meet enough people in these industries who are so full of themselves and who seem to feel a sense of entitlement to this unnatural life of luxury, you begin to wonder how they are possibly qualified to determine how much they think you should pay for laundry detergent. The entire spectrum of retail prices is just about how much their competition charges against how much they charge, and it has nothing to do with how much the product is worth to the consumer. Generally, their estimations are off-base, so they then flood the market with coupons and rebates. That means those of us who are good consumers end up getting the product for free or for a profit.

It is my belief that if the products were simply offered for sale at market value and were made of a decent quality by American employees our country would experience a vast turnaround in a short amount of time.

I know: one sentence is too short and simple to get to the root of the problem, but there it is. Globalization is good for some things and bad for others and the main thing it is bad for is our civic pride. How do you have any civic pride when one of the only things setting your community apart from any other is your hockey team?

HACKTIVISM

Every tree-hugging ideological teenager feels that way, but of course they are such extremists they want to distinguish themselves by boycotting anything "commercial," making each other rich by imitating the process, gradually migrating to cities and opening up bakeries and charging $5 for a cupcake. This does not improve anything; it just mirrors the problem because in time even the most cosmopolitan city street will look like the corporate shopping mall the rest of the country looks like, since chain stores go where the money is. These kids are trying to hide from the malls near where they grew up, generally located in rural or suburban areas, but that's no way to beat them. "You can run, but you can't hide."

If a Wal-Mart opened and all anyone bought was the loss leaders and *nothing* else, the place would be out of business in months. Why is that nearly impossible to do? Well, it would require people communicating with each other and planning to do it! How is a whole community going to communicate when most of the venues to do so have been wiped off the face of the earth, replaced with machines for social interaction, and our unnatural shame and fear of talking to strangers in a grocery store? I don't know.

Fear not, there is one place left where social interaction still rules; it's the one place where you're not supposed to communicate verbally at all—the public library. I have met so many fellow coupon shoppers using the computers at the public library. In order to print out more coupons than we're allowed at home (the print-at-home coupons have a restriction on them based on your IP), we just go to the library and print out multiples of what each person needs and then exchange them.

Coupon shoppers even have their own underground currencies, such as postage stamps and formula checks. These are used as payment for other coupons and goods that were acquired for free using coupons. Some days I feel like we are living in some sort of bizarre post-consumer secret society.

REFUNDING MAKES SENSE

For those who live in remote areas with no access to good coupon promotions, there is rebating (or refunding). It's a whole other world.

There are four main publications dedicated to rebating: "Refund Express," "Refund Cents," "Refund World," and "Refundle Bundle".

Of the four, the oldest and most informative is "Refundle Bundle," although to be honest, "Refund Cents" has a more active trading community. That is to say, if you're a beginner, you should really start with "Refundle Bundle," and once you have learned the ropes, get an additional subscription to "Refund Cents." For some reason, none has particularly good websites and there are an ever-changing group of coupon websites which offer some, but not nearly as much information about refunding.

Refunding magazines are like a clearinghouse of the available promotions that are currently being offered by all sorts of manufacturers. They read almost like catalogs, with long, cryptic lists. Each magazine even comes with a sort of "decoder ring" that you use to decipher the sometimes hundreds of obscure abbreviations in each listing.

So what is the purpose? Well, for many of the items you already buy, the manufacturer is most likely offering a rebate or full refund of the purchase price to help promote that item in a certain market where it is not performing as well as the competitor. To advertise this offer, they distribute rebate forms to be displayed in local supermarkets.

Unlike coupons, which may be void if transferred, rebate forms themselves have no cash value and it can be quite lucrative to, say, trade the "$5 rebate when you buy t-shirts" form you got in Ohio to someone in California for the "$10 rebate when you buy winter gloves." This example is exaggerated on purpose— people in California rarely need winter gloves, hence the need to solicit to them. To transfer the form into Ohio where people are most certainly buying gloves (which are probably on sale due to the competitive nature of such a staple) creates a great opportunity for people in Ohio who need to buy winter gloves.

Often the rebate exceeds the purchase price of the product, creating the opportunity to make a profit. A great one of mine was a deal from Walgreens in which I purchased 177 bars of Ivory soap for $5 using coupons during a sale, and then got a $25 gift card. The promotion required you to purchase "$100 worth," and the key word there is "*worth*." That does not mean you have to spend $100, it means $100 *worth* of product must scan, but then you can coupon it down however you like and the rebate is still perfectly valid. I have not had to pay for a bar of soap in over two years; Ivory was already the brand I was using and I made $20 taking it all.

Here's a cornerstone of rebating which is easy to get you started and can save you 50 percent on meat, one of the hardest things to save money on. Beer companies are notorious for rebates in states where it is illegal to rebate beer purchases. We have seen forms like $25 when you buy $50 in meat. At the time there was a deal to get a box of Omaha Steaks' hamburgers delivered for 96 cents, which you could do over and over again. We placed 55 orders, and then used the invoices for the rebate, getting the Omaha Steaks at around 25 cents a pound, delivered via UPS, and our cat had a field day playing with a living room full of Styrofoam coolers (I think she tried to perform the stage version of "Pink Floyd – The Wall" with them.) You could also just go to a local butcher and buy $50 worth and ask them for a proper receipt other than a cash register tape, which may not have their name and phone number on it.

We even got a rebate on a pair of U2 concert tickets once. The cheap seats were $54.50 and when we did a 30-day trial of some online program which paid Ticketmaster an affiliate commission, they sent us a $25 rebate, bringing our tickets down to $42 each. Sure, we still had to pay the crazy service fees, but it was a discount on a normally premium priced item nonetheless.

People who tell me they don't do mail-in rebates always have the same story— they tried once and they never got the check. When I ask if they called the rebate company to find out where the check was, the answer is always no— they lost the form, they forgot, they never followed up.

Free money is all over the place in the rebate world: all you need is a pen, paper, and a little organization to stay on top of what is due to you and when and it's all yours for the taking. Jump on in, the water's fine.

REBATE FRAUD

Just as you have to watch out for wasting money buying magazines and products to help you "save money," with refunding there is also an incredible amount of fraud and illegal activity, which can be a real deterrent to the beginner. Since it is such an incredibly easy and profitable way to make money, it attracts an element for which it was not intended, a type the serious refunder would have no reason to engage in illegal activity with.

In the past, there have been "rebate conventions," which, like any other civic meeting, involved a variety of discussions and activities, but were used only as a front for people to trade qualifying forms, proofs of purchase, and receipts. Since most rebates are limit one per address, the criminals constantly had to trade multiples in order to maximize the amount of income they could make. Transferring refund forms does not generally invalidate them, but transferring forms *along with the materials needed to redeem them* is certainly fraud, since the person submitting the form didn't actually purchase the product.

Some people have gone so far as to create computer software to generate random cash register receipts, which could then be programmed along with the qualifying purchase included on each receipt. The bogus receipts were then sold for around 50 percent of the rebate price so that people who had acquired the proof-of-purchase on the package by some means other than buying the product (like digging it out of your neighbor's trash) could still request the rebate. Obviously, this is blatant fraud, and is bad not only for the manufacturers and the rebate houses, but for those of us who legitimately redeem mail-in rebates. When it becomes that easy to dig money out of the garbage, problems obviously will occur.

It's a lot of work to make a few dollars illegally when if you just follow the legitimate promotions laid out by the very same companies you can make so much more money with so much less work. I don't tell you about these problems to scare you away from rebating, but to make sure you're on your toes when you get into it. Coupons are simple and friendly, rebates are very profitable, but just be careful when you get started because there are certainly going to be people out there trying to get you involved in illegal activity. You need to understand what is going on so you don't make some naïve blunder and then discover you have broken federal laws in the process.

WHAT THE "EXPERTS" WOULD TELL YOU

For a moment, I would like to compare this technique to what you will often read about from sleazebag publications like "Bottom Line Personal," and "The Home Economizer," or from the "Coupon Queens" on television, as we've already discussed. In any of those examples, a soap deal would probably require taking as many trial sizes as possible when staying in a motel. They would probably also tell you that motels are cheaper than hotels but as my friends can tell you, it's cheaper to stay in a five-star luxury hotel using a good travel deal than it is to stay in a Super 8 no-frills motel where the scenery will make you want to ingest some really heavy drugs and listen to Johnny Cash records until checkout time, which is printed in bold red letters on every other surface of the room.

All of the "professional cheapskates" I have met own boxes full of small soaps and shampoos they have taken from motels; the only ones we have are from the Four Seasons and the Polynesian Resort at Disney World (normally $450 a night, we paid $175). Wait, that's not true, we stayed at one luxury hotel which featured Bath & Body Works soaps and shampoos, so we cleaned out a whole housekeeping cart of those.

Otherwise all of our toiletries are store-bought— the usual brands we already used and liked that were either free or we were paid to take. I have never read a single article in "The Home Economizer" about that, probably because they are too busy filling the pages with leftover casserole recipes and suggestions of piss-poor modern family films that everyone in your home will "enjoy." You want to see a really good family film that everyone will enjoy? Good luck. They're very hard to come by, which is why portable DVD players are so popular.

That leads us to another real problem with rebating which we don't have with couponing and that is the amount of money involved to get started and be involved. Each of the publications I have mentioned costs money and some, like "Bottom Line Personal," cost a whole lot of money when you consider that most magazines may be subscribed to either for free, or perhaps $5 a year. They promise to help you save money, but charge you a lot for it. It has been my experience generally that most of them are simply not worth it. "Refundle Bundle" is worth it for at least one year because it is like paying for a lesson in rebating and that is a good education to have. You can learn all the same things for free online, but here it has been compiled for you in an easy to understand manner. As much as I taunt the publisher of "Refund

Cents," her publication is useful up to a point, but I am not sure if it even justifies the price tag.

Just like with everything else, all of the information you need and want is available for free online if you look for it. You would never know that from reading the books and articles published by most of the other people mentioned here because all they do is try to steer you to their website to sell you more things. Some of the things are of value and some are not. We may sell things in the future, but they are all original, all designed to entertain and inform, yet none of them are truly essential to learning how to save money.

EVERYONE IS AN EXPERT

No doubt you have heard the sarcastic phrase "everyone is an expert," and this is never truer than after someone has completed a good rebate for the first time. One of the most famous rebates in the last couple of years was for five free portable DVD players at Radio Shack.

Here's how the deal worked:

On December 23, 2005 only, you could purchase an Axion DVD player with a 3.6-inch screen built-in for $129.99. There were two rebates, the first for $70, both available only on 12/3/05, the other for $65. In total, these rebates were for $135 against a purchase price of $129.99, which meant you would make $5.01 per unit before tax. There was a limit of five units per person, per household.

For a couple of brief hours in the early morning of that day, the Radio Shack website actually showed the total price of -$5.01 after rebate and I made sure to print a copy of the screen in case the rebate was disputed later.

I coupled this deal with a coupon for 10% off any purchase of $40 or more at Radio Shack, and paid $116.99 per unit before tax, thus bringing our profit to $18.01 per unit, with a total profit of $90.05 just for walking the units out of the store. We could have thrown them in the trash and still made money.

So what happened later in the day?

People who had never done a rebate before in their lives ran into Radio Shack first thing in the morning and put somewhere in the neighborhood of $650 on their credit cards, got home and decided that before they cut the UPC symbols off the boxes, (thus making them non-returnable), that they should call the toll-free number on the rebate form just to verify that they would in fact be receiving a refund.

Neurosis and rebates do not mix.

Even though the rebate clearly spells out the offer in writing, even though the website clearly showed a total price after rebate, even though there was ample recourse for the consumer should the rebates be fraudulently denied, some people still decided to call the toll-free number and speak to some miserable person working in a call center in Minnesota a few hours before Christmas Eve to ask if the rebate was "real." If you ask a dumb question, you're going to get a dumb answer.

And that dumb answer was "no" —that was what was reported in the media. After enough amateurs called enough news desks, the story spread like wildfire. I sat there watching a deal I had done that morning on the network news in complete disbelief. Didn't a single reporter bother to read the rebate forms themselves? This was such a simple deal; sure, it was profitable, but it wasn't complicated at all. There was no conspiracy, no fraud, nothing illegal or even immoral. Heck, Radio Shack actually selling something of value for a fair price was indeed a news story, in my opinion, but that wasn't the story they were interested in presenting.

I shrugged because now the rebate processor would have more reason to get the rebates mailed out faster, but they came 12 weeks after the sale as promised on the rebate form.

Just two months earlier, a new website called "The Consumerist" had formed. Not only did they fail to report this deal or any of the hype surrounding it, they had yet to even begin this kind of hear-say journalism.

Everyone interviewed on television that day was an amateur; anyone with any common sense could have read the rebate and understood that there was no cause for alarm. The people who caused the whole phenomenon were the ones who got excited, whipped out their credit cards, and then panicked.

This is only the first half of the story. The part which was completely ignored by those same news outlets was that two months later, on February 17, 2006, Radio Shack announced a 62% decrease in their fourth quarter earnings (that being the quarter in which the DVD players were offered), and decided to close between 400 to 700 retail stores which they claimed were "underperforming."

At this time, Radio Shack had in excess of 4400 stores and the store I visited had 15 DVD players in stock. You do the math—because the news media sure as hell can't.

THIRD MOVEMENT

"SHOP THIS MESS AROUND"

IT WASN'T ABOUT THE SOUND

When Parliament Funkadelic first decided to abandon their look as a Doo-Wop group, one of the first decisions they made was that the sound they were producing was not nearly as important as the overall feeling the audience should receive from the performance, "the vibe," as they called it.

There were two key elements they designed to help generate "the vibe" at their performances: the first was to dress in psychedelic-style clothes which were associated with newer rock and roll bands as opposed to doo-wop groups. This also had the added effect of addressing the audience, most of whom were dressed similarly to the performers, whereas in doo-wop the performers were dressed in a flashier manner than the audience who was attending the show.

The second was to have an absurd number of people on stage at any one time, even if each performer was doing as something simple as shaking a tambourine, because it created the illusion that the group was indeed a group of people, and not simply a few people. This group was like a party; therefore if a concert had no audience at all, nobody on stage would care or even notice. But if there were an audience, they would all feel a part of something larger than themselves, one of the most primal reasons that people attend music performances in the first place. Most importantly, if the actual music was terrible (most of it was), or if the performances themselves were terrible (most of them were), nobody would even notice or care. The entire show was much more akin to performance art than it was to a music recital.

With these two elements, Parliament Funkadelic were able to attract artists in a variety of mediums to contribute album covers, short promotional films, stage sets and costumes.

Parliament Funkadelic were so successful at what they did that within a couple of years a more commercial version of their sound began to become popular and in 1974 the first disco song reached #1 on the Billboard charts. Whereas the funk asked people to be true to themselves (in manner of dress, in spoken dialect, even in terms of body odor), disco was all about escapism. The mecca of disco was Studio 54, a club famous for excluding more people than it included (some nights there would be lines down the street to get in and only a few people inside). Disco was perceived to be extremely elitist and as such in December 1977, a full year before disco reached its cultural peak, Parliament Funkadelic issued "The Pinocchio Theory" (performing under the working group name of "Booty's Rubber Band"), a song which explained that much like the fictional character Pinocchio, if you "faked the funk" your nose would grow. This was a double entendre, as persons who enjoyed the disco culture were stereotyped as indulging in the use of cocaine (cocaine abuse often leads to swelling of the nasal septum).

This isn't to say that disco wasn't a phenomenon or that it lacked artistic merit; there were many disco acts who were clearly talented musicians, but during this period Parliament Funkadelic became more popular than they had ever been before or would be since, playing arenas nightly with a stage set that featured a spaceship (named "The Mothership," another double entendre) landing on stage.

So why did people remain faithful fans of funk music and why did it actually increase in popularity when disco should have put it out of business? Because it felt like a family, a true cultural movement that stood for something. It continued to pick up momentum based on its ideals of racial equality, racial identity, and dropping acid while painting your face with Liquid Paper (while disco's only ideal was "lets have a good time").

Marketers have stolen this concept, "faking the funk" as it were, promulgating the idea that a brand name is a family name and asking you to "join" their family.

Social networking sites such as MySpace or Facebook may even have pages started by brand names as if they were people, which you may add to your list of friends. You wonder if some zombie is sitting there saying, "That's my brother Doug, that's my wife Tracy, that's my best friend from high school Rob, and that's Febreeze, I use it to deoderize my car every day."

It's typical to see marketing copy such as "When you purchase our item, you become a part of our extended family." No, I don't. I become a customer of your shitty product. The only familial aspect in the transaction is that we are going to fight like cats and dogs when the thing doesn't work and I want a refund.

One day last year I got two invitations in the mail: the first was for a family function, which I threw in the trash, and the second was for a free Delta Crown Club one-day pass. I kept the one for the Delta Crown Club pass. Had they invited me to be a member of their family, I probably would have thrown that in the trash too.

Recently, Delta Airlines rented a retail space in New York City and called it "Delta 360." As a Delta passenger, they emailed me an offer saying that if I visited this location I could exchange a printout of the email for a free one-day pass in their lounge at the airport. I arrived to discover a room designed to look like the interior of an airplane, where you could sit in the new seats they had installed on the planes to see how comfortable they were. Free beverages were provided and there were enormous bowls filled with individually wrapped snacks.

On the same day, Coca-Cola had rented part of the space to promote its beverages in conjunction with a basketball tournament which was taking place at Madison Square Garden. Outside, Coca-Cola was giving away cans of its Minute Maid brand juice drinks and a parade of German tourists wandered past and stuffed their pockets with cans of juice. Then they came inside and took the complimentary Delta shopping bags and dumped the bowls of snacks into them. There was free wireless Internet provided and not one homeless person in sight. If you walked outside and looked in any direction, the sidewalks were littered with packets of cookies which had fallen out of people's pockets as they walked away.

While I appreciated the free food, it is my belief that travel is equally miserable on any commercial carrier in the United States, and that I will continue to fly on whichever airline where I can book the cheapest ticket. While I understand that advertising and payroll are not directly related, it is still absurd to me that the airline rented an expensive space in Manhattan, sent out tons of advertising, gave away tons of free club passes and food, and then a few months later began to cut 4,000 jobs from its workforce. The sound at Delta 360 is one thing, the vibe is another.

FAT WALLET

Fat Wallet was a website where people would announce deals they had discovered and then everyone else would either comment or help contribute to creating a clear set of instructions on how to get the same item at the same price. In the process, you use FW's affiliate links for the various retailers and they give you a portion of their commission. In effect, both you and FW earn money from your own shopping and when you get items for free that is called free money.

Everyone is encouraged to participate, with the goal of making themselves rich and loaded with free merchandise; FW is encouraged to continue providing a forum for these conversations since they are profiting off the sales being made. Ideally, it is a win-win situation.

I spent three weeks on Fat Wallet before I ever bought anything. Most of the conversations were so hilarious; I was laughing all day long at the antics of people and their quest for free merchandise. One of the first topics I remember reading was about a guy who had found some 26-foot aluminum ladders at Home Depot for a penny. He had figured out that there were a few minutes between when an item was marked for clearance and when the clearance price kicked in, a window in which the price would adjust to one cent. So there he was on the screen with four yellow aluminum ladders strapped to the roof of his compact car, holding up a receipt with a 4-cent total, smiling for the camera.

For several days I read about his antics until finally I couldn't take it anymore and had to walk down to Home Depot and see if it was all true. At the time I had been very sick and didn't leave the house often, so the fluorescent lights and noise of Home Depot were very disconcerting. To add to my problems, for some reason my medication was making certain surfaces appear absolutely terrifying to me, and the concrete floor at HD was practically making me climb the walls.

It was the middle of winter, so the selection of barbecue grills was extremely limited, and they had put heavy chains and locks around the base of each to keep people from trying to move them. Looking at them sent a chill up my spine. Then I heard the noise of something scraping across the floor which had been causing me to panic in the first place. A man was dragging a $600 stainless steel grill across the floor and he asked me to help him. After explaining about my health and apologizing that I couldn't help him, I asked what the story was. He told me he had three minutes to drag the grill to self-checkout because it was going to ring up for a penny.

He gave up but we stood there and talked for quite some time about the whole Fat Wallet thing, and then we went across the street for a cup of coffee. Apparently, he too had been following the thread about HD clearance and had started trying it himself recently. Supposedly, he had found a few items at the one-cent price, but he heard they were "cracking down" on it. Who knows how much of what he was saying was true, but I was intrigued.

MANY RIVERS TO CROSS

The next day Jean had to travel on business and I was left to my own devices for a weekend. When she came home Sunday night, she could tell something was wrong, but didn't say much. Five minutes is about as long as I can keep a secret from her, so I had to tell her about the awful thing I did while she was away. Most women would fear some kind of infidelity in this situation, but not her, especially when it took me 15 minutes before I could even stand up (because I had been sick in bed at the time). No, what I did was even worse than infidelity; I had ordered 600 bottles of water to be delivered the next day to our two-bedroom apartment. Yes, it could be worse, we could live in a studio apartment, but considering I was barely strong enough to pick up a bottle of water, never mind a case of it, it was a particularly bad situation.

I couldn't help myself after reading the deal on FatWallet. A bizarre adrenaline rush somehow forced me to order enough Poland Spring water to fill our living room, kitchen, dining room, and bathroom.

Staples was a store that I never shopped at before reading FW, mostly because everything seemed so expensive. Since learning about Staples' deals, I pretty much shop there every day, even on vacation. Back to our bottled water. So I spilled the beans and Jean flipped out, and rightfully so. I had no business ordering 600 bottles, which would probably put a hole in our floor and end up in the basement. We called Staples immediately to cancel the order but we were told it was too late; they had already packed it up for delivery. But they told us to tell the driver when he arrived that we wanted to refuse the shipment, and Staples would credit us.

About an hour later, I got ten emails telling me that my order was confirmed and would be delivered tomorrow. What I quickly discovered was that the order had been placed ten times. When I clicked on "Checkout" I got an error message, so I did it over and over until the order went through.

The next day, as promised, a big red truck showed up at my front door filled with (and I wish I were making this up) six *thousand* bottles of water. When I explained to the driver that it was a mistake and I was refusing delivery, his eyes popped out of his head and he cursed me out before damning me to a lifetime of eternal thirst or something and then he got back in the truck and drove off.

Let's explore the deal itself: 600 bottles of water delivered was $100. A coupon for $20 off a purchase of 100 or more was applied, the new total was $80. The order was placed via FW, which then gave me $2 in commission fees for the purchase, making my new total $78. Then we used our Staples Rewards card, which pays back an additional $2 in store credit, effectively making my new total $76. Next we paid for the order with a Discover card, which at the time was offering five percent cash back at Staples, so that's another $4 off, making the grand total $72. My total was about twelve cents per bottle, at which price bottled water is finally cheaper than gasoline, a rare occurrence.

After two weeks, I still didn't see the credit on my card so I called Staples again to inquire and they apologized and placed me on hold. The customer service representative told me she had credited me back a thousand dollars for the ten orders. Something was not right with that; I realized that my card had only been charged $800. When I explained to her that the coupon had somehow gone through ten times and that I only paid $800 she put me on hold again, and after what seemed like 30 minutes the CSR told me I should just keep the refund credit because they couldn't figure out how to process the return for the correct amount.

To say I was stunned is an understatement. For the first time ever, I had just made $200 for doing absolutely no work and simply *refusing* to accept a product from a well-known retailer manufactured by a well-known brand. This was almost a full week's paycheck if I had been working a minimum wage job, made for absolutely nothing at all.

From that very moment I was hooked and have not looked back since. There was no false pretense, no deception, no theft, nothing, a company just said, "Here, have 200 bucks cash thanks to our inability to use our own point of sale system." Well, okay, if you insist!

Seconds after hanging up the phone, I was back on FW to brag about my first big score, when I discovered the conversation about this deal had ballooned to almost 30 pages. A majority of the people who ordered the water received it and were now discussing how to make the deal better. That's right, they paid for and received a product at a substantial discount and now wanted to figure out how to make it even cheaper. So what were the brilliant ideas? My favorite involved another $30 in cash back after you drank the water and returned the bottles for deposits. From there, people realized that most states do not have deposits on bottled water, so next we were all involved in figuring out per mile how much it would cost to transport the empties to Michigan where they would credit us and if that was financially beneficial.

My good fortune was greeted with cheers of victory by other members, but I noticed that a week later people were still discussing it and I had no idea why. It turned out that the next week (this was a full three weeks after the deal) Office Max had the same water on sale for $80 but without a coupon, which meant you could call Staples and price-match after the fact to the Office Max price and get another $22 credited back to your card (the difference plus ten percent of the difference).

Conversations about the water deal continued for a full 31 days, until you could no longer return or price match it, at which point it just fizzled out.

OH LISTERINE,
WHY CAN'T YOU BE TRUE?

These deals often occur in the most unexpected ways. A few nights later I was in terrible pain and couldn't sleep, so I rolled over and turned on my laptop to discover at around 3:00 a.m. someone had just posted a new deal for Listerine. Listerine is a staple around the house and it can be very expensive, so this posting had piqued my interest. The author of the post laid out the basics: go to the Office Max website, use a coupon code, and get one gallon bottles of Listerine for 25 cents. Having just weathered the storm from the bottled water, I decided to play it cool and order "just" four bottles. Four one-gallon bottles of Listerine are of course bigger than our bathroom cabinet, but this was a real deal I could use and at the time I felt it would save me around $50.

After placing my order, I sat back and let the action continue. It's kind of like participating in a story that keeps unfolding. We all know when we are getting sucked into something and for a moment I had horrific visions of myself dressed up like the guy on TV in the green jumpsuit with the question marks all over him.

Within 24 hours some people had claimed to receive whole pallets of Listerine already, with a couple of them talking about how they had it put in the garage next to drums full of body wash from a deal they had gotten in on previously. Short of running an orphanage or homeless shelter, it's pretty hard for the average family to use up 30 or 40 gallons of Listerine in a few years, so what were people going to do with all of it? Resale is normally the first thought, but since it's a heavy liquid, that can be cost prohibitive. A discussion began about what to do with it all: some suggested using it on the lawn to kill weeds, while others suggested it was a homeopathic remedy for certain sexually transmitted diseases. Others refuted that claim, suggesting they had tried to treat themselves with it previously without success.

Then people started refuting the theory that it could be used for any of these purposes, just as most of us were reporting that our orders had been canceled. A "false alarm," as we call it in the biz.

Relief was all I felt when the order had been canceled: I no longer felt any stress about where to put the stuff, what to do with it, or having to explain it to Jean. It's easy to become hasty and impatient when you're getting involved with these deals for the first time.

But then I began to wonder why the order was canceled. In most lines of business if you have given the merchant your credit card and it has been charged and you have received a receipt for your purchase, shouldn't they then be obligated to deliver the merchandise at the price offered?

Technically, just about every state will allow a refund in full and call it a day, but this presents a larger problem that I do not feel has ever been truly investigated by any consumer affairs department.

Most websites will have a clause in their terms and conditions stating they are not responsible for pricing errors, which I feel is completely ridiculous, how is it that they aren't responsible for their own mistakes?

These "false alarms" seem to happen quite frequently. A desirable item is offered for sale on a website at a substantially discounted price, followed by a post on Fatwallet or Slickdealz discussing this offering. Many people place orders, receive confirmation, and then days later receive a cancellation notice after the website realizes they can't possibly sell this item at the advertised price.

In a court of law, you would have to prove that there is a pattern of behavior to show that it is intentional and I'm sure if you mined the past four or five years of Fatwallet you would probably find one or more merchants engaged in this behavior. It is my belief that some companies may be using this practice either to increase the size of their mailing list or perhaps to profile "demon" or "devil" customers. All I can say for sure is this: no matter how good a deal looks, until you have the merchandise in your possession, don't count your chickens before they hatch.

IT JUST BE CALLIN' ME, LIKE IN THE MIDDLE OF THE NIGHT

My friends were still calling and laughing at me for the bottled water incident, when yet another deal came up. When I signed up for that Staples Rewards card, I was mailed a variety of new coupons for things I had never expected. One of them was a $10 off $10 or more at the Staples Copy and Print Center. Back on FW, I asked people what to do with the coupon since I didn't need any copies made and they told me to go have a self-inking rubber stamp made for my return address, the stamps cost about $11 to have made, so with the coupon they would only cost $1.

ALL DEALS MUST PASS

Another person jokingly said, "yeah and pay the dollar with Dealpass." I wondered what Dealpass was and so I did some research. Dealpass is a program to which you pay a membership fee and are then allowed to purchase gift cards to major retailers at twenty percent off face value. The trick is that you can't just go to the website and join; you have to be "invited" from another website, either by purchasing something or perhaps joining a mailing list. The Dealpass program is often re-branded based on the website that "invites" you, so perhaps if you bought a DVD at "Sam's Video," then after you check out a window pops up inviting you to join "Sam's Discount Club" or something like that.

There is a limit to the number of cards per year you can purchase at the discount, so your first inclination is to buy the limit in one month and then cancel your membership to avoid paying a high monthly fee, which could negate the discount over the course of a year. I have personally never really done this because as soon as I look in my shopping cart I think "Wow! Do I really want to spend $3,000 at Target in one year?"

While I'm sure that I probably do spend $3,000 in a year at Target, it still seems really crazy when you look at it in one lump sum, and so I always chicken out, buy a couple hundred dollars' worth and then cancel the membership.

No matter what you do, the deal is useful because it creates a discount on items to which no other discount may apply or to which so many discounts may apply that people would look at you with a degree of concern and say "you're sick" when they see the total at checkout.

HOW TO GET PAID

Just about every week, Staples will sell antivirus software free after rebate. There are two main brands of antivirus software— Norton and McAfee. Each software is free after two rebates— one for buying the software and the other for "upgrading." In the list of qualifying products that you already own for the upgrade each will list "any product by [the competitor]" as qualifying. One of the more common coupons Staples distributes is $30 off $150 or more.

The math goes like this:
$75 McAfee software
$75 Norton software
$30 coupon
_____

$120 out of pocket

Now you're going to ask me how to get the qualifying product for free; well, you just did. You simply use the proof of purchase from the McAfee to qualify for the Norton upgrade rebate, and you use the proof of purchase from the Norton to qualify for the McAfee upgrade rebate.

-$120 out of pocket
+$150 rebate checks
_____

$30 cash profit

Congratulations, you have performed alchemy by turning a worthless slip of paper into real money, legally, ethically, and all it took was about five minutes of paperwork. Now let's get into it further using the tactics we learned from the bottled water. First, we are going to order the software online, not in the store and, yes, you generally may use these coupons online. So FW is going to give us about $3, Staples Rewards another $3, and Discover another $7.50. Our new total is going to be $43.50 profit.

We have another option here to consider which may be more profitable. Since Staples does not accept gift cards online, we could go to the store and pay with the Dealpass cards. At a twenty percent discount, our profit now skyrockets to $60 on the purchase of the two software boxes.

Usually at this point of the conversation, people start to get confused and ask me about what kind of software it is and what it does. My reply is *who cares*? By the time you're done cutting out the proofs of purchase and

UPC symbols the software boxes look like Raggedy Andy had a rough night at a biker bar, so they are pretty much useless for gift giving or resale. About the only thing they are good for is recycling, so send them to recycling. Thankfully, everything in the package can be recycled so it won't end up in a landfill. Charity thrift shops are full of five-year-old antivirus disks covered in dust priced at $10 because they look "new" and "valuable."

SCHOOL SUPPLIES

Schools are a huge money waster. In one page I have taught you how to avoid paying for deodorant ever again, which in theory could save you thousands of dollars in your lifetime. Go ask your kids what they have learned about saving money in school. Not much, of course, and that's because a good number of the teachers themselves are absolutely awful consumers. I know quite a few teachers and only a handful are people I know from coupon shopping. Teachers always want to tell you about how important it is to change kids' lives, but that is often motivated by their deep psychological problems. You should practically demand to see the teacher's checkbook and if a teacher in 2009 or later actually opens a purse and shows you a paper checkbook with a written register, then you know they are completely worthless. Why on earth anyone needs to carry a checkbook with you is beyond me. This means they do things like pay for groceries with a check and that is such a sin against mankind; I don't think it's too strong to say they should be hung from a flagpole. Especially working with children! It's horrific.

You can also use the Dealpass cards along with price-matching on loss leaders to absolutely kill any chance that they will see a penny from you on the sale. Every year back-to-school shopping starts earlier and earlier and the competition gets fiercer and fiercer. Price-matching, as I have explained, is the policy by which one store will match a competitor's advertised prices on an item either before or for a certain number of days after you have purchased it. Since during back-to-school shopping all the stores are selling the same items, it becomes very easy to stock up on free school supplies.

The idea is to buy the items when they are full price, then price-match them to the competitor. With the 10 percent bonus on the difference, and paying with Dealpass cards, you're sure to stock up.

Here's an example:

Week #1

Staples is selling composition books for $1.99 each

Wal-Mart is selling composition books for 25 cents each

Buy the book at Staples for $1.99, but paying with a DP card which means you have paid $1.60 out of pocket.

Go back to the customer service desk after your purchase at the register (remember, if you price-match before you buy then you don't get the extra 10 percent) and price-match to Wal-Mart; your credit will be $1.91 placed back on your Dealpass card.

The 25-cent book has now cost you 8 cents of "gift card balance," which is about 7 cents of real money. This means you can buy three of the books for less than a quarter.

When September rolls around you can watch in disbelief, as I do, when parents invade every office supply store they can find, filling their carts with things like $1.99 composition books and paying with their debit cards. And as you know, I feel that many teachers and education administrators just piss away money by telling you how expensive it is to stock up on supplies. So many parents seem to live in a state of anger because teachers demand these long lists of supplies that are "so expensive," but the fact of the matter is that in July and August the major retailers are begging you to take these products off their hands. Why don't teachers give students supply lists for next year at the end of the previous grade as opposed to the first day of the current grade?

We did a radio show about this once where I asked our listeners to send in the supplies lists from all over the country and we compared them with the supplies lists that were being given out at the stores. Then we called some teachers and asked them to justify some of the supplies that seemed excessive, and they were all honest and reasonable people who justified each item on the list. That was a bit of a surprise to me, but teachers do plan well and try not to put anything on the list that they do not feel the kids will really use. However, when I asked them why they didn't give the supplies lists to the parents at the end of the year, all of them thought I was crazy. When I explained how we got school supplies nearly for free none of them had ever thought of it.

Math, English, Social Studies, Science, heck, even Physical Education are all good and important classes for children to take, but what about "common sense?" What about "finance"? Math is not finance; it's a component of finance. There used to be Home Economics, but by the time I took it all we did was bake cookies and sew. I keep saying it over and over hoping someone will listen. By senior year, students should know how to calculate an APR and know what a credit card fee disclosure is. We all know that most will never use Algebra or Trigonometry in real life, but they will use credit cards every single day. I just don't get it, and it makes me mad.

Using these methods to buy school supplies at a discount of 95% or more is a great example to set for your children and a great way to teach them both mathematics and basic finance. Try it, what do you have to lose?

I started to find myself at Staples every single day. Our apartment was literally overflowing with stuff we would never use and were having trouble even giving away. Our postman started turning down the electronics I was trying to pawn off on him because he said his wife threatened to leave him if he brought another cordless phone or universal remote home from work.

Down the street, I started trading office supplies for coffee and donuts at the coffee shop every morning. My desk at home was so cluttered that I would take my laptop and cellphone down to Staples, along with the coffee and donuts, and use one of the display desks in the back of the store as my office for a few hours each day. It made things easier when there was an in-store deal posted on FW; since I was already in the store I didn't have to waste any time driving there. A few months later they started airing commercials on television featuring a man doing the same thing I was already doing. He was doing it just once, but I did it every day. The employees would have kicked me out but I used all the coupons and free Staples money to buy them all sodas and snacks from the store display cases; that way if the manager told them they couldn't accept anything from a customer they could say that it was purchased from within the store and "good for business." Not only did they put up with me, they started hanging out at "my desk" to see what deals would happen next. Nobody could believe how crazy these offers were. I turned shopping at Staples into a "part-time job" complete with a "staff." Best of all, when I would get free merchandise I could barter it online and then ship it right out from the Staples store since they have a UPS counter right there.

In six months I never had a single argument with a store manager until one told me it was "enough" and I had to "leave." Not wanting to be accused of trespassing, I packed up my things and went home. I wrote Staples a letter explaining how rude it was that he treated me so badly, especially when "I was a really good customer who shopped there every day."

Days later he was either fired or transferred to another store and I was back to "work." My heart was no longer in it, though; I had proved my point to myself and learned everything I wanted to learn from the experience. A couple of days later I decided to stop hanging out at Staples every day.

BETTER RUN THROUGH THE JUNGLE
(BEFORE ALL THE GIFT CERTIFICATES ARE GONE)

Back over on FW another deal had been posted and this one required my immediate attention. Sign up for AOL with a 30-day free trial and receive a free $100 Amazon gift certificate, yours to keep even if you cancel. Sounds good, right? It gets better, though, since there was a typographical error which somehow allowed you to sign up over and over again. The phone calls started coming fast. "How many did you get? I've made over a thousand bucks already!" was the first thing someone shouted at me in the frenzy.

Now at the time, nobody had heard that stupid recording of the guy trying for 45 minutes to cancel AOL, since it was not really news to any of us. Collaborating our techniques, within a few hours we all had figured out ways to cancel quickly, but admittedly some of the earlier phone calls were hilarious. Any reason you gave to cancel, the customer service reps would say "that is not an acceptable reason for you to cancel." If you could manage not to laugh too hard, you could then just keep saying "I want to terminate the account" over and over again until they finally did it. Of course, the professional FWers had already solved this problem by paying with "virtual credit cards," which are a feature at some banks.

Virtual credit cards work like this: let's say you were ordering something over the telephone from a company you had never heard of and you were uncomfortable giving them your credit card number. The virtual credit card program would allow you to log into your bank's website, tell them how much you wanted to spend at this store, and issue you a fake credit card number (which deducted the money from your account, and could only be used once) to use at that store, which could only be billed up to the amount you specified. You would then give this fake credit card number to the merchant instead of your real credit card number.

In this case, should the customer call AOL and be refused cancellation, (since the advertisement clearly said you could cancel within 30 days at no penalty) they would have recourse to ensure that AOL upheld its end of the contract.

By the time it was all over we were sure someone at AOL must have gotten fired and most FWers were buying all their Christmas presents over at Amazon. It would be at least two years until one guy somehow ended up all over the news trying to cancel his AOL subscription, and you could tell this guy was a total amateur because if he was not getting anywhere after five minutes all he had to do was call his credit card company and have them process a chargeback.

That's one of those things in the bargain hunter community: people want a lot of credit for discovering deals, but they don't want it in the mainstream press because the sheer number of new people it would bring in would then kill the deals much faster. Of course, I remember this from indie rock in the '90s when nobody wanted their favorite band to become too popular, or it would be harder to see them in smaller clubs and the ticket prices would escalate. Elitism has truly hit the mainstream.

COMPETING DEAL SITES

After a few months on Fat Wallet, I wanted to branch out and see what other deal sites were out there. I figured they must have competition, but Fat Wallet prohibited anyone from discussing any of the competition on their message boards. Fat Wallet welcomed our radio show and let us use their server to broadcast until someone called in and started giving us the names of other websites that did the same thing FW did and maybe better. The next day Fat Wallet no longer took our calls and cut off our access to their server. How naïve I was to think that when FW said it wanted everything to be for the good of the community, it meant the community on its site only.

I couldn't figure out what they were so afraid of. At the time, I thought FW was the only site that offered cash back, so I figured you go to these other sites, get the deals, then use FW for the cash and they would still make money off you.

As it turns out most new users at FW fall into the same trap. They feel locked out from any other site to discuss bargain shopping, so one of my first ideas—and still one of the most popular pages on our website—was a list of all the other deal sites out there I could find. I knew that if I was looking other people were too.

It was hard to make a big list at first because each site follows the same structure; they don't want you talking about any other sites so they can keep you active on their own. This seemed extremely hypocritical to me; you have a website to discuss consumer choices in obtaining the lowest prices, but you don't want the consumers discussing which forum is the best to discuss these choices. Since I was not interested in advertising revenue, I felt it would be no problem for me to post a nice list to give those consumers as much choice as possible. Along the way I discovered some great websites and many other cash back programs. My favorite discovery was a website called evreward which let you bargain shop among the cash back sites, so if you were buying something from Sears you could go on evreward and compare what percentage of cash you would receive from either FW, eBates, Big Crumbs, or many others. The percentage difference was staggering and it always changes merchant to merchant, site to site.

Since then we've learned that this is the problem with almost every deal site out there. Since many of them exist to make various commissions or advertising revenue, their entire goal is to keep you within their realm and pretend no other sites exist, even deleting any references that are posted to any competing site. Surely this is not in the consumer's true best interest and it wouldn't be so infuriating if it weren't sold as being the complete opposite, as if they were offering you advice on how to get the best deal.

One of the most common ways you learn about other websites like this is from getting a private message from another user suggesting that you check out such and such website, a very primitive form of viral marketing.

I followed one lead to another, until we started to settle down on these websites that talked more about saving money on groceries and everyday products than electronics and office supplies. I know it sounds weird because the first two deals were bottled water and Listerine, but most of the deals on FW are things that require electrical outlets or batteries.

AND SO YMMV RADIO WAS BORN

This was an interesting shift in dynamics on the message boards. You had FW with its perceived fat guys in leather chairs buying up everything in sight, and you had the coupon sites with all of these submissive housewives on prescription drugs fighting with cashiers over free Hot Pockets.

We had started doing the radio show around this time and were very lucky to be welcomed with such a great reception. The phone started ringing off the hook for days on end with people wanting to talk coupons and deals. All sorts of characters were coming out of the woodwork. A lot was happening all at once. Mostly, people were telling us about their own experience rather than asking for any kind of insight or advice.

The floodgates opened and we began to learn about all kinds of websites where deals were discussed and people traded rebate forms. There was even a "Star Wars" themed website where you had to discuss everything in "Star Wars" lingo but all the deals and coupons were based here on planet reality.

SO-CALLED "EXPERTS" OF THE DEALSITE SCENE

There are two kinds of people the media turns to for information regarding deal sites (usually on Black Friday, the day after Thanksgiving, which is reported to be the largest shopping day of the year). The first are people who are selling something under a guise.

Examples would be a website which has "deal" or "savings" in its name and lists what it considers to be "good deals," few of which truly are, and all of which have affiliate links, (i.e., that the owner of these websites is getting paid a commission for every sale.) It is my personal opinion that these sites are potentially harmful to the end consumer and should be looked at more closely by the companies offering up affiliate accounts, but then again they are generating income for the same companies, so why would they bother?

The second place the media turns is to consumer affairs blogs, most notably "The Consumerist," a website run by people who have no experience in consumer affairs. A majority of the information posted on the site is hearsay, with little, if any, proof of the allegations included with the accounts of poor customer service. Why is this site so popular? The site is owned by Gawker Media, which is funded by a dot com millionaire, not quite the "organic" growth that is assumed with the blog medium. Gawker can afford publicity for The Consumerist, while real consumers with real complaints cannot.

So why do the media turn to these two places? Because they are sensational, easy to find, and can be bundled into 45-second news pieces. What is the problem with that, you ask? The problem is that it distracts from the real consumer news which is not being reported.

If you want to learn how to save money on groceries for free, simply open any web browser and search the words "COUPON FORUM." You will find what you're looking for, free of charge.

THEY CALL IT "CENTER STORE"

On these new message boards we were learning about things like free deodorant and free tampons. It was much smaller scale, but these were items we really needed, not just items we wanted. Here we were able to get down to the bottom of grocery pricing and in the process we learned a lot about how we as American consumers are raised on packaged food. Now before you go burying your head and thinking, "Oh shit, this book is gonna go downhill," don't worry, I'm not about to go on some hippie rant about macrobio, renewable fuels, or anything else like that. You can still wear shoes with laces, it's okay. But if you want a real lesson in the economics of a grocery store, try buying food for your family for one week without buying anything packaged, frozen, processed, or prepared. It will change your life.

We discovered this completely by accident when we were in Connecticut doing research for a project. I got really angry at my friend Alex for not paying attention to the merchandise in the store. We would walk into a store and he would spend an hour looking at fruits and vegetables while Jean and I were filling the cart with free cookies. I told him we could not talk about comparison-shopping produce on the show because produce was a variable, unlike a box of Chips Ahoy. The New York box of Chips Ahoy is identical to a box of Chips Ahoy in California; the product is the control and the price is the variable. With lettuce, you now have a variable product and price, so it was impossible for us to discuss on the show whether it was a value.

From here, we spent almost two hours in the breakfast cereal aisle and we compared what we ate every day and which products we used on a regular basis. Now I had known Alex for a long time, but you really get to know someone when you have a conversation like this. You see, Alex eats almost no prepared or packaged food, which may or may not be healthy (I'm not a doctor), but it IS a complete departure from those of us who subsist almost entirely on packaged or prepared food. This is where the organics people step in and tell you about how healthy organics are, but I am not on that kick. Having spent four hours at a Whole Foods Market with Alex looking at items like organic dental floss, I personally feel that a majority of that trend is just

that, a trend. Again, since I am neither a doctor nor a scientist, I am not qualified to tell you what is truly healthy and what is not, but I do know I can get
Stop & Shop's house brand of dental floss for free with a coupon and organic
dental floss costs over $3. I personally haven't noticed any medical or dental
problems as a result of using Stop & Shop's free dental floss.

Another thing I finally figured out in the course of using these smaller
and more focused message boards was that it may not really be in my best
interest to contribute to them, but instead to make friends, exchange phone
numbers, and then have an uncensored conversation with other people
either on the phone or in person. During a normal day, I usually speak to
about eight people on the phone who I met entirely on message boards to
discuss shopping in one form or another. While I often have to repeat the
same stories eight times, the quality of the conversations and the information we exchange is much richer and more useful than anything I have ever
read on any message board.

JEAN SAYS MY BALLS JUST FELL OFF

While I have never seen it in print, and certainly not by a professional of any
kind, it seems to be just common sense that message boards are in fact very
addictive. The ability to "hang out" and wait for someone else to say something for you to respond to appeals to a lot of us, but it is not a proper sub-
stitute for social interaction. Just as children should be forced outdoors to
play in the dirt with other kids from time to time, maybe we should have
enforced playtime, too. There have been whole weekends where Jean and I
sat in the same house at separate desks and just hit refresh over and over
again. Once we realized we were doing it, we both said it was absurd and
now we almost never look at the message boards when both of us are home.
Life is too short to waste it reading about other people's drama. (By the way,
if I didn't say it earlier, thanks for buying this book.)

Talking to stay-at-home moms (SAHMs) every day really became
another life changer for me. I would be typing away on next week's show

while in between coupon trading and deal discussion I would hear all the PTA drama, and the housekeeping, cooking, or dealing-with-playdate drama. Eventually I ended up being a SAHS (Stay-At-Home-Sam), but because I was childless I was only taking care of a cat and preparing for Jean's eventual return from work each evening.

For us, the couple who used to eat Mexican takeout on the sofa every night or wolf down hot dogs next to a garbage can at some sports arena, the radical transformation into a SAHS means that Jean comes home to a three-course candlelit dinner with music every night and that all the dishes are done before we go to bed. Previously, we had a solid four-year run in which every single dish or fork was paper or plastic.

"Refund Express" published an article by a woman who had a college degree in Home Economics, and I began to completely idolize her. The humor here is that during 2002 I saw the Rolling Stones almost 40 times and often woke up in hotel rooms in a pile of newspapers and receipts, with half a cheeseburger on my pillow. Now I keep searching high and low for Rolling Stones oven mitts.

While I do not necessarily always believe in the SAHM/SAHS lifestyle, I have allowed myself to be involved in it up to a point so that I can better comprehend the stereotype of the typical American housewife in relation to shopping habits and patterns, and for this I am eternally grateful.

One of my first get to know you gambits was to ask people to send me photographs of the food and supplies they had stockpiled in their homes from the various sales and promotions they had partaken in. The results would have sent a diabetic into a coma. Some people had entire basements full of instant mashed potatoes and frozen bagels. You had to see it to believe it.

On the homefront, I was slowly learning to prepare meals with fresh ingredients, clean corners of the bathroom I never knew were dirty, manage the art of meal planning (although I do it very poorly because almost every meal involves chicken), and learn about neighborhood groups. But the key element of being a SAHM is creating the perception to both your spouse and children that you have everything under control and making it look like you've spent your whole day preparing for their comfort upon arriving home.

Let's face it, the definition of "homemaker" is incredibly sexist. Is it really socially acceptable for a woman to spend her whole day essentially working for her husband and children while her husband is out making money to support the family? Granted, this could be an agreeable partnership but once we assign genders to the roles it becomes sexist. Men can be just as good homemakers as women, and I don't think most women doubt this, but the men doubt it; they find it demeaning or embarrassing to do these jobs and that is nothing short of crazy. Since intentionally becoming a homemaker to Jean, our cat, and some stuffed animals, I can assure you that the job of "homemaker" is twenty times more difficult than most of the high-paying jobs I have held in my lifetime. When I chat with "the girls" on the phone, a majority of them are on anti-depressants or anti-anxiety medication —is it any wonder? This is an extremely complicated and physically intensive job with no pay, no possible promotion, no breaks, and almost no recognition. The problem is that if you're doing the job right, it should be impossible for anyone else to notice, so the claims of "but you don't do anything all day" turn out to be a sick sort of compliment. Only a man could have invented such a fucked up career and then insisted that it was a job only fit for a woman.

Right now every woman reading this book has intense interest in what I am going to say next and every man is thinking, "Fag!"

No, I'm not gay, but what I am is taking a serious look at the pages of *Better Homes & Gardens, Good Housekeeping, All You, Redbook* and most of the other "women's" magazines. If you ran the text through a word processor and replaced the word "Woman" with the word "Black" and the word "man" with the word "White" you would have such insanely racist copy that I'm sure even the Reverend Al Sharpton would have to question if violence were the wrong way to respond.

The articles generally talk about nothing more than how to make everyone else happy while reserving the "little luxuries" for yourself, which are miniscule compared to the output everyone else demands of you. In my opinion there is no balance, or equality; instead, you get just two pages of sexual advice geared towards his pleasure and not your own. It's disgusting. Luckily, here in New York City most women read this stuff and groan or ignore it, but the readership of these magazines is huge and on a national level if even one percent of the readers believe the content there is something horribly wrong.

Now I am not some kind of feminist-loving-man-hater; it's still a man's job to bring a woman flowers on a date, but that doesn't mean she should be seen and not heard. So many men I know still basically think the goal of marriage is to enter into a contract whereby the woman will cook, clean, run errands and have sex with you in exchange for not having to "work" all day. They also believe that black leather sofas look "elegant" and go nicely with framed panoramic photographs of Las Vegas or New York. I've owned plenty of black leather sofas and panoramic photographs of Las Vegas, so trust me, I know what I'm talking about here.

Coupon and rebate message boards have been a real disappointment in this area. Both have strongly reinforced the fact that so many women truly believe in these magazine articles stereotypes. I have seen posts where women talk about going to classes in order to learn how to be more submissive. They are horrendous and with my big mouth, I have had to let them know how I feel about these classes. Sometimes you can see the whole system breaking down and the way it affects the whole family's health.

Obviously, you can think back to television and print ads from the 1960s where the manufacturer is stressing to the housewife about how a product will make her job "easier." Most of these commercials are funny now because you can see how ridiculous the product was relating to the task at hand, but what is *not* funny is the fact that commercials today do the same thing with equally ridiculous products and yet most people don't find them funny. Wipes are the best example here, as you can buy just about any kind of liquid cleanser in a "wipe" form, which is a pre-moistened paper towel sprayed with the cleanser so that you no longer need to spray the cleanser and then wipe it up, saving you mere seconds of time and shelf space because you don't need to store a spray bottle and paper towels, just the can of wipes. It's the stupidest product ever, and it produces no great time-saving ability. As you can imagine, based on volume, wipes are considerably more expensive than just buying spray cleanser and paper towels.

People love these stupid wipes, they fly off the shelves, and every two minutes another one is put on the market, and every time someone uses one they feel the need to utter "I love these wipes!" You can now purchase wipes for every part of your body from your mouth to your ass; they make wipes to clean the counters, the windows, your car, your cellphone, your computer screen, everything. Soon there will be a wipe to clean the outside of the containers the other wipes come in and people will buy those too.

But let's return to the topic of SAHMs and to one of their favorite topics—nutrition. It would be very 1970s of me to tell you that more and more SAHMs take their kids to McDonald's after school instead of preparing them a snack because it is simply easier and more convenient, so let's skip right over that and go right to dinner, which is the quintessential meal for the stereotypical housewife.

Dinner consists of a well-rounded meal centered around the food pyramid designed by the FDA. Nobody knows exactly how many servings of what you're supposed to get a day and it is actually kind of hard to figure out from the FDA website, although I have tried to look into it many times myself. If you were a "super-housewife," you would probably know the whole chart backwards and forwards, but I am clearly an inferior housewife.

So basic logic says you should have a protein, a starch, something with fiber, and perhaps a little sugar. In English I am saying meat, green veggies, potato or bread, and something for dessert. This is really easy to do using fresh ingredients and it might take you an hour or so to prepare from start to finish. Using coupons and rebates we generally have this dinner every night for about $2 per person or less.

When I take an informal survey every day of what the SAHMs are making for dinner, they're usually trying to stick to this formula but working with the items they have couponed down, such as frozen vegetables covered in a cream sauce, or using a combination of prepared foods that are fairly unhealthy. The SAHMs know that the products are generally not as healthy but they also know that five minutes in the microwave using disposable containers they don't have to clean will truly help them save time and money so on the table it goes. Sometimes this is not even the food they want to serve but what has been requested by the family so it makes their job much easier to just serve it and keep everyone happy. I don't need to preach about fast food, but I'm sure if they made a meal from scratch it wouldn't be so much turned away as met with utter shock.

There's also the issue that many people simply don't know how to cook, so the prepared foods make it easier for them at least make it look like they do. Let me be honest. As an honorary SAHM, that's a lame excuse and you need to do your job right or you need to quit. You're bringing the rest of us down. Yes, I said the SAHM value system was sexist, but if you're doing your job, you have to do it to the best of your abilities; otherwise, you're reinforcing the negative aspects (i.e. you're making it more believable that your job is to just sit at home doing nothing while your spouse makes money), and that's wrong.

VIDIOTS

I don't always buy into the food choices SAHMs make regarding what is okay for their kids to eat. Knowing as much as we do now about food marketing and food additives, it seems almost criminal to let children consume unlimited amounts (or virtually unlimited amounts) of many of these products. But I hear from parents time and again that children beg and plead for these products by name since the marketers have used the kids as virtual soldiers fighting a war against their parents' pocketbooks and decision-making abilities. Now I have to admit I haven't witnessed this first-hand, but I hear it's extremely powerful stuff. What I never understand is why parents can't sit down with their children and explain exactly how the various forms of marketing have convinced them that they need these products.

And this comes from someone who yells and screams and obsesses about getting a new videogame every Christmas. And yet I haven't played a videogame for more than five minutes without getting bored in well over ten years. I don't really want or need the game, but I can't stop thinking about how much I want it and how it will "change my life." Part of being a modern adult and an educated consumer is understanding that you have these impulses and knowing they are unreasonable and need to be kept under control until they pass. And they always pass just as soon as a marketing campaign for a new product begins to capture your attention.

Usually, though, if I really think about it, I can in fact determine why I feel the need to buy a product. Just about anyone can; it just requires you to be truly honest with yourself, something which very few people seem to be anymore. Why be honest with yourself when your anti-depressant/ anxiety/stress/aging medication allows you to remain deluded?

CAMERON DIAZ IS PROBABLY UNDERPAID

One summer there was a print campaign that featured Cameron Diaz holding a cellphone behind her back; posters and billboards of this image were everywhere. You try getting any heterosexual man to avoid staring at Cameron Diaz's ass at any possible opportunity. As a result, I personally own a $200 cellular phone that I didn't want or need just because the advertisement featured Cameron Diaz holding it against her ass.

Chances are pretty good you own just as useless an item for just as stupid a reason.

When your children tell you they "need" something new, sit down with them and talk about why they "need" it. Teach your children how to be honest with themselves and dissect the marketing. Many of you may already do this, but I believe that the majority of parents clearly do not. This is yet another extremely important life lesson which is not being taught in grade school.

Some of you are thinking, "so what? Who cares if my children grow up to buy a lot of stuff, what's wrong with buying lots of stuff?" Clearly, you've never heard of the "No Child Left Behind Act," which requires schools to submit names and birthdates of your children to military recruiters. The armed forces employ the same marketing agencies as the companies that make products. If your children can't understand how marketing works they're going to be extremely susceptible not only to squandering their income but also to a great deal of personal trauma. I am not against the armed forces in any way, shape, or form, but I am horrified by some of the tactics that are being used to recruit teenagers who don't really understand what it is they're volunteering to do.

THEY COULDN'T CALL IT "WORST BUY," COULD THEY?

Down the street from Staples was an institution of continuing education known as Best Buy. Why not start hanging out there?

My first job as a teenager was computer repair, so I was interested to see what Best Buy's "Geek Squad" did for the customer other than humiliate their employees by making them wear ridiculous outfits and drive obnoxious cars. Mostly, what the Geek Squad does is charge you for every move they make. Taking your computer to the "Geek Squad" is like being a patient in a teaching hospital; a number of the kids working there appeared to me to be learning as they went along.

They charge you to do things like install the software you just purchased in the store. If the task of opening the software package and following the two or three steps is so daunting that you feel the need to bring your computer to the store, wait in line, and pay upwards of $30 for someone else to install it, might I suggest you shouldn't be in possession of a computer at all?

AND IT LOOKS LIKE IT

In areas of the Best Buy with more technical product, my experience has been that I found it difficult at best to find a member of staff to answer any questions. A great example of this is the aisle full of hard drives and blank media. Let's face it, most people want to know the difference between a DVD-R, a DVD+R, a DVD-RW and a DVD+RW. This is going to be one of the most common questions in an aisle full of the media at full retail prices, which are generally far above what most others charge. For the extra money you're paying, common sense suggests that you might get a salesman to explain the difference and help determine which product is right for you. Nope. When I visited the store there wasn't even a simple sign explaining the difference in the four formats, which is naturally what ninety percent of the customers are going to ask. Here's a fun game: Go look up on Google what the four formats mean, print out the information and put it in your pocket. Then walk around Best Buy and ask the employees what each of the four format abbreviations means. You'll rarely get the same answer twice and if you produce the printout they'll say, "Wow! I didn't know that, you must be an expert!" or something equally stupid. I mean, what the hell are you paying for at that point?

One time I saw a guy returning an open package of DVD-R discs that were incompatible with his system. The customer service rep actually opened the box and counted every last one to make sure they were all there. Now they can't resell the open box because he may have damaged a few trying to write to them, but they counted every last one as if the guy were some kind of criminal trying to pull a return fraud. The poor guy only bought the wrong ones (at full price) because he didn't know any better AND there was no one there to help him.

A couple aisles over there's more blank media, with some other formats like videocassettes and minidiscs thrown in for good measure. The prices are completely different and the packaging is different, but it's all the same product. Whilst it may be a mistake, I wouldn't be surprised at all that people fall for this on a regular basis. Today I saw a four pack of blank DV cassettes for $19.99, but right next to it in the photo section were packages of two tapes for $6. This past Black Friday they were selling them for 50 cents a tape, but there was no rush to buy them. Bins of them sat around all day while people lined up for hours to buy flat screen TVs for a couple dollars more than other merchants sold them for online.

WHY DO GROWN MEN SLEEP ON A SIDEWALK OVERNIGHT IN ORDER TO PURCHASE A VIDEOGAME?

We all know someone, maybe even ourselves, who has trouble dealing with reality. After all, we're all human and lots of bad things happen to us no matter who we are or where we're from. Each of us has different coping mechanisms— mine is humor. Yours may be religion, alcoholism, drug addiction, false idol worship, overeating, sex addiction, codependency, gambling, collecting Hummel figurines, or, if you're like most men between the ages of 18 and 45, it's video games.

Video games have become so involved and so realistic that they can feel like an escape from reality so intense that it is clearly an addiction. For those of you who may be unaware of this, put down this book and spend 30 minutes at the local Gamestop and listen to the conversations grown men are having. "I'm in training for Madden (insert next year here)," as if they're actual football players on an actual football team in training for next season (and in a really sick way they are). Too bad they're not exerting any physical energy and when they win at the end of the year they're still fat, lazy, and sitting around the house with a plastic videogame controller in their hand.

The last sentence of the previous paragraph is the part that they never seem to realize; it is also the most important.

There are video game simulations of any imaginable scenario available, not unlike pornographic videos; for both of these the target consumer is (laughably) in the same demographic.

Find the sword in the castle, land the plane on the runway, kill the monster with the laser gun, park the car in the garage— they all follow the same premise in one way or another. The really sick ones are like the various "Sims" games which have no purpose, no goal, no task; they're just virtual online communities in which to "hang out." Strangers look at you like you're crazy in the coffee shop when you introduce yourself and stick out your hand to shake, but they think it's perfectly reasonable to spend over two hours online pretending to be a person in a virtual coffee shop without making eye contact or exchanging any physical language. Now does this sound like a group of mentally and socially healthy people to you? Setting aside the fact that half of them are probably medicated to the gills, do you think they make up a group of people qualified to spend money in a retail environment? But they are the people who spend *the most* money in a retail environment. The subliminal excitement of seeing and touching real things makes them forget about value and quality. When you intentionally live half your life online in this manner you have become so disconnected from humanity that you're bound to be taken advantage of, and stores like BBY are ready for you. They see you coming a mile away.

LIFE IMITATES ART, POORLY

I spent almost six months hanging out at BBY every day for an hour or two in order to get a sense of who shops there, why they shop there, how they make and spend their money, and what they spend it on. One day I walked up and saw two police cars outside the store. I asked the loss prevention guy what was going on and he said that a high school student had stolen about a dozen video games (they average $50 a piece, so he was stealing over $500 worth of product). When he approached the exit and security tried to stop him, he bolted, knocking the two security guards down and running into a getaway car. Instead of taking off, as the security guards came out, four men got out of the getaway car and began to beat the crap out of the two security guards; only then did they get back in the car and speed off.

The symbolism, whether intentional or not, is remarkable. A disenfranchised teenager robs a store that sells games they know he cannot afford yet market to him that he "needs" to buy. The store itself sells them in a style not unlike that of a football video game, to which the thief responds in the same manner as he would respond to a football video, when the store attempts to retaliate just as it would in a football video game, his accomplices then further retaliate against the store for trying to penalize them for breaking a real law. But the only way the store can sell the otherwise worthless product in the first place is to rely on its own marketing campaign to inculcate in customers this desire to be distanced from reality. The product itself is software on a plastic disc, essentially a 25-cent item. Further compounding the irony and symbolism is that if the thief had been reasonably educated in computer literacy by having played enough of these videogames, he could have found a simple way to get a pirated copy of the game without any violent means and without ever having to leave his home. While I am not advocating the piracy of intellectual property, what I am saying is for a criminal, he was a really dumb criminal, and yet a perfect BBY customer had he had any money to spend. He believed in the mythology so strongly he was willing to risk his own freedom for it. If that doesn't scare the pants off you, then you must be not just knee deep in it already.

A LACK OF TALENT IN THE LABOR POOL

As I have already said, prerecorded music was BBY's main loss leader, the ruse to get the "young and hip" crowd into the store and then try to slam them with overpriced gear to play it on. That doesn't mean they did the job very well, since any record store clerk can tell you it takes a good deal of musical knowledge to stock the shelves correctly. Never mind the fact that, just as the blank media aisle is devoid of sales staff, so is the prerecorded music department. This is amazingly typical when you realize that the music department probably takes up the largest footprint of any area in the store except for the televisions. There are usually two or three employees who are stationed in prerecorded music, video, and videogames. It is nearly impossible to have a thorough product knowledge of even two of the three, and that's if you had an IQ over 150. When you consider that the inventory is huge and there is almost no copy depth (the number of multiple copies of the same title on the shelf at any one time) on anything catalog (catalog titles are any titles which are not new releases), you would need two Kevin Smiths just to staff the prerecorded video section alone.

So how does this affect the average consumer? Let's say your friend tells you about a great movie you never heard of (it doesn't matter what the title is). A BBY has opened in your town and put the local video store out of business. While you could order the movie on the Internet, it's a Friday, you just got paid, and you'd like to see the movie this weekend when you have time. Pretty normal scenario so far, right? Okay, so you go to the BBY and you can't find the movie anywhere. The DVDs are sorted by very general categories such as "Action," "Drama," "Family," "Comedy," etc.

In a privately owned video store, the clerks know which section your movie is in because they have had to stock the shelves, and, chances are, if they're movie people they have probably seen it already. At a BBY, they throw the stuff on the shelves wherever it fits so long as it's in alphabetical order (another huge challenge with this crew). Just in case a district manager walks through, he wants to see that all the movies that start with the letter "C" are in the same general area. "Terms of Endearment," for example, does not belong in "Family," but the employee thinks it looks like a family film from the picture on the cover and puts it there anyway. If you can't find a movie and you can somehow manage to find one of the three employees, the first thing they do is ask you, "what kind of movie is it?" How the hell should you know, you haven't even seen it yet!

Then they go through the routine I have already described in which they walk right back to where you have already looked and don't find that a copy has magically appeared there either. In my experience, the next step is to walk you to the bestbuy.com kiosk to look it up, where the first question is always, "what's it called again?"

I mean, they have a painfully simple job that they are either too lazy or too stupid to perform properly. At the very point of the potential sale, they couldn't even remember for all of one minute the title you were looking for. Who's to say they could remember it while they were looking at the shelf?

When I tell them the title, there is a seventy-five percent chance they will misspell it as they type it into the computer, and after you've corrected them, once they find it, all they are looking for is what genre of picture it is so they can go back to the shelf and look again. Invariably, they can't find it, and end up telling you that it can be "special ordered."

If you ask the clerk to check the in-store inventory and it shows up, yet you can't find it on the shelf, there's a little game you can play. You play this game partly because you just want to buy the movie and get out of the store, but partly because at this point you want to get even with them for wasting your time. Here's the trick: as soon as the clerk walks away, use the kiosk and order the movie for "in store pickup." Within minutes you will see the same employee scouring the shelves, ripping them apart, looking for your movie. You can sit back and watch in amazement and as soon as they find it, rip it out of their hands and take it to the register yourself. They will panic thinking that another customer has already bought it. Don't worry: if you don't pick up the order (and no need to because the line at customer service is even longer than at the register) your card won't be charged and the order will be canceled in a week. So why did the clerk work their ass off as soon as you punched in the order? Because then corporate could see how long it took to fill the order and that can affect these imaginary numbers which are posted on a bulletin board for every employee to see. The management probably either congratulates or scolds the employee like little children in daycare based on what these numbers say.

WORSHIPING THE DEVIL CUSTOMERS

In November 2004, the CEO of Best Buy, Brad Anderson, made public his intent to categorize Best Buy's customers as either "Angel" or "Devil." "Angels" were the customers who paid full price for everything, and "Devils" were the ones who were bargain shoppers.

Based on a supposedly new business theory at the time, the "devils" were costing the company so much money that just by finding ways to discourage them from shopping at the store, the profit margin would increase almost automatically overnight.

When you think about it, it's pretty funny that the store is called "Best Buy."

In the three years that followed this decision, Best Buy has been profitable and whereas I used to shop there daily, I might go twice a year now.

No matter what Mr. Anderson thinks about "firing" his "bad" customers, let me assure you that the "devil" customers do in fact have the place on a string, and it's so easy to make the staff and management dance like puppets at a moment's notice once you know the things that motivate them. These imaginary numbers on the bulletin board are their number one motivator. Sales are irrelevant and profits are irrelevant because just by doing *nothing more devious* than walking into a store and attempting to buy a specific product that *they sell,* you can absolutely torture them and cost them a fortune in lost time by simply demanding that they find the item. I mean, do you think a system this crazy really deserves your money?

What CEO could go out and publicly say that they wanted to sell every product at the highest price possible to the most ignorant customers imaginable and get away with it? Brad Anderson, that's who. The formula— to put as many ignorant people as you can in a room filled with overpriced electronics— is an inspired work of genius.

CAMCORDER DISORDER

I could talk about all the people who purchase camcorders needlessly at Best Buy all day, but let me summarize by saying this:

If you have ever or would ever videotape a public fireworks display, then you do not need to purchase a camcorder.

FIGHTING BACK BY MAKING THEM PLAY THE IN STOCK SHELL GAME

Remember my solution to finding a movie on the shelf? This can be used to get a really great deal on small appliances. Go to the store and find the appliance you want; look for one that is sold out but still shows one unit available in the system. This is pretty easy on weeks when something like a freezer is on sale; since the sale starts on Sunday, go to the store on the following Friday when you can be almost positive it is sold out. The salesman will tell you it's sold out, but over at the website kiosk it shows "available for in-store pickup." Simply order it for in store pickup and a few hours later you will get an email stating that the item is sold out in the store and instead they'll ship it for free, if you like. Great, you get the item on sale, plus Reward Zone points, plus credit card points, plus online cashback, and with free shipping. Since BBY does not use UPS to ship small appliances, they will absorb the delivery cost and you get a great deal. Don't hesitate to price-match if you see the item on sale at Sears the following week.

Of course, the main reason for tricking Best Buy is because they are trying to trick you. It has been reported correctly in the media that Best Buy has two websites, which are identical except for prices. The one with the lower prices can be reached from outside the store and the one with the higher prices is accessed in the store. The reason for this is so if you come in to the store and say "hey, this item was $9 on line and you charge $12 for it here," the salesman can say, "let's go look at the website together." When he shows you the item is $12 on the website, you'll think "oh, I guess I was mistaken." It's a variation on bait & switch (which is illegal in many states), done with a new edge—i.e., website vs. paper catalog. All one has to do then is walk the salesman over to the Apple section of the store, where the wireless cards are built into the demonstration laptops, and just switch over to another wireless network (perhaps from the coffee shop next door) to demonstrate that the price is in fact $9 on the website.

In this basic example, you're using all available tools at your disposal to counter the manipulation being used against you by the retailer.

MAGNOLIAS ARE TOUGH TO AVOID BEING EATEN BY BEETLES

There is no question that I am a real "film snob"; I freely admit that. But even when I'm watching French Film Archive prints of Jacques Tati's *Playtime* in

16:9 on DVD I do not need a $10,000 television. Hell, I don't even need a $1,000 dollar television. The movie looks amazing on my $500 DLP projector which is a real luxury to me given it's the most expensive television I've ever owned (and I own over 2,000 movies on DVD and VHS.) Do you think the average consumer going in BBY needs to blow ten grand so they can watch *Hitch* starring Will Smith? Every time you go in to one of these places they always show the same lousy movie like *Independence Day* in the highest definition. I mean, when Warners launched pre-recorded DVD product the premiere title on display at retail everywhere was *Space Jam*, a steaming cinematic pile of dogshit (and I am a HUGE "Looney Tunes" fan who saw Jordan play on the dream team in person twice, once at courtside. Yet I still wouldn't fork over $500 back then for a player in order to watch *Space Jam,* just as I won't fork over $10,000 now so I can watch *Hitch* in high definition and high fidelity. I have recently discovered that *Space Jam* is one of the most rented films on iTunes. What the fuck is wrong with people?

About a year ago someone gave me a BBY gift card and I was in need of a new DVD player for my then-new projector. Since I watch so many foreign films, I knew I needed an up-converting DVD player that would play DivX movies and be region-free. Units like this were available all over eBay, Amazon, Buy.com, and every other major online retailer, so I just assumed there would be one over at Best Buy. Nope. Technology changes very fast, but BBY's purchasing, marketing and supply chain don't work nearly as fast. Nor do Circuit City's, but my point is this: if you're looking for truly new technology you aren't going to see it in any major brick-and-mortar chain for at least six months until after it has hit the market. By the time it hits those stores there will be a clearer sense of how popular the item might be and its corresponding price. I bought the DVD player for $199 and just about six months later a comparable unit finally appeared at Best Buy for $399. Why not offer it as soon as it hits the market? It's less profitable, so why even bother to let the consumer know it's available? It's just like the portable Compact Disc players, only in this case you don't even have a choice—they simply don't offer it. I'm sure they will but only after the units cost $10 on eBay and BBY can finally charge $80 for them and make a healthy margin.

LIKE FLIES ON SHIT

When you're a teenager, feeling cool is really important. We've all been there, we all know what it feels like. You're never going to feel cooler than when you get your first job. You're making money, you feel smart, and as if you're in demand. The ultimate in teenage egotism is telling "old" people what to do and feeling like you're somehow profiting from their "stupidity." This is why the retail staff is so young— it's almost cult-like in nature. They all have to be drinking the Kool-Aid for it to work since it's just a big façade. While I could write an entirely separate book about how this works in truly urban areas, for the moment let's talk about how it works in its main demographic, which is rural and suburban areas.

We all know the stereotypes of the quarterback of the high school football team being super-macho and popular while dating the head cheerleader. Other than John Wayne as a cowboy, this is probably the most stereotypical American image in our culture. You also have the "smart" kids who move away and go on to college and make a ton of money. But what about everyone else? We have this whole spectrum of people who feel left behind, stuck in twelfth grade with no future.

Here's what the problem is with the BBY environment: it creates false hope, it creates a false solution for those who feel left behind. Instead of motivating them to do what feels right to them and helping them to live their own lives to the fullest potential, it traps them in an imaginary society and culture in which they will consistently be replaced by someone younger and eager. The terminated and older employees will no doubt be more bitter and less encouraged than they otherwise would have been, and will become adults who waste their money trying to buy back their youth and the "good old days." You know how powerful nostalgia is.

None of this is consistent with human nature. A whole country of children on Ritalin, Xanax, and Zoloft graduating high school without enough education to open a checking account, working at Best Buy as shills only to get fired sounds like a miserable future to me, but that's where we are at the moment.

The employees all buzz around the sales floor in a testosterone-fueled frenzy, buzzing like bees on their cellphones, with no sense of separation between reality and imaginary, some truly believing that the release date of a videogame is a significant moment in American history and acting accordingly. So many of the workers take and make calls for the stores on their personal cellphones because the lines between personal life and work are so intentionally blurred. Some even use phrases like "let me check with my guy," as if they are mechanics in their own shop needing to order a part. The naivete and self-destruction would not be nearly so painful to watch if you didn't know that it was all being communicated in a flashy and appealing way intended to get these people to put on a show for the greater benefit of the shareholder.

Each time one of them offers to sell me an extended warranty for $15 on a $20 item and tells me what a good value it is, and you look in their eyes and you can tell they really believe it I just want to scream "HELP!" Maybe next time we can all scream together.

So why have I just said so much about Best Buy without discussing any other big box retail chains in as much detail? Because they're all the same. Practically all of these stories could have been applied to anything from Home Depot to Payless Shoes. It's the absurd structure and its lack of function that I want to convey, not the specifics of each and every chain. But I will tell you one great fact about Payless Shoes that you never read in the press: pimps are among their best customers. Pimps will go in a Payless and clear off a rack of women's shoes because, just as in any other business, pimps want to keep costs as low as possible.

FASHION: A WOMAN-ON-WOMAN HATE CRIME

I swear to you, the saleswoman thought I was a transvestite. I stumbled into BCBG and was apparently asking far too many questions about the women's clothes for a straight man writing a book about shopping. This kind of thing happens to me all the time, but it was apparently quite a big deal in this store where in my view the staff gave the impression they believed they were selling haute couture as opposed to the mass-produced, overpriced shit that they peddle.

Maybe I was being overly inquisitive because I had just spent 20 minutes in a boutique that sold nothing but very elaborate $15 outfits for pets, or maybe it's just that I simply can't believe how many people fall for this stuff.

Now, I'm not some hippie loser bitching about how you should wear earth-toned rags all day and cover up your body odor with patchouli, nor am I so ignorant to think that fashion designers aren't true artists, but you aren't buying their work, you're buying mass-produced reproductions of it. There's a difference between owning a real painting and a Thomas Kinkade.

When it comes to women's fashion, men never notice what women are wearing unless it is overly revealing, you are trained from birth that how you look on the outside says a lot about who you're as a person, and after looking at the clothes in 90 percent of these stores it seems to me the target customer is trying to say that they sleep with other people in exchange for money.

Some woman outside BCBG tells me that the store is "the new Bebe," and I ask her if she knows who Charlotte Russe is. She replies, "Oh, she's like a really famous designer," and when I inform her that it's the name of a dessert she thinks either that I am kidding or that it is a "super-coincidence."

The clothing options for men are no better: either you wear a suit or you're apparently expected to wear a "surfer" outfit purchased at Hollister, Pacific Sunwear, or any other of the multiple imitators which exist within the mall.

In the past few years, most of the popular fashion has aligned with either "surfers" or "skaters," an utterly ridiculous concept when you consider that if even half the people wearing these clothes actually engaged in either sport there would be lines of cars six miles long to get near any beach or skate park at any given moment. So why do so many people wish to emulate these lifestyles?

The last time a skateboarder looked cool was when Christian Slater was in *Gleaming the Cube,* and that's going back almost 20 years, and the surfer is still epitomized by Sean Penn in *Fast Times at Ridgemont High*, the very same stereotype repeated some 20-odd years later in *Finding Nemo*, a children's movie.

The surfer stereotype is of a dumb, well-meaning, friendly person out to have a good time. And this basically describes the modern customer who is looking to emulate this stereotype. BCBG is quite proud of the fact that celebrities such as Paris Hilton and Lindsay Lohan, both described in the popular media as rather dumb "party girls," shop there. We all know that a fair share of teenage girls are looking to emulate the party girl image, and let's not forget the parade of teenage boys looking to be gleeful idiots when they grow up.

Mind you, at least for the boys, all of the stores sell jeans and t-shirts, almost all of this crap is made in China or Indonesia, and almost all the price points are the same across the board. Is the girls' clothing more expensive? Of course it is. And do the parents give into it? You bet your ass they do. The parents claim that the kids will be tortured by their peers in school for wearing the *wrong* clothes, that their kids won't have any friends if they don't dress them in these current trends, and that being shunned could affect their child's mental health and self-esteem.

Good, try it and see what happens. Your children may grow up to have no self-esteem, but they'll have significantly more self-esteem than the children whose parents fell for all the marketing.

When you inquire to the various corporate headquarters of these chains as to the logic behind many of these decisions, you're told that the brand is a "lifestyle brand." As such, you can find a lifestyle brand in the marketplace for virtually every kind of lifestyle except your own. Lifestyle brands exist to goad the consumer into believing they can become a part of a culture which they aspire to, not necessarily that they belong to. You had better believe it costs a lot of money to change lifestyles every so often! If you live in the suburbs of a landlocked state, you don't have any business dressing like a surfer. It is the adult version of a child proclaiming "I AM A SPACEMAN!" and making an astronaut costume out of commonly found household items, only it's more expensive and more delusional.

Tons of functionally illiterate young adults spend large amounts of their parents' money at Abercrombie & Fitch, a lifestyle brand which advertises an "Ivy League" look, yet many of these customers couldn't get into a community college (nor could they find it without a GPS). The store even looks like a teenager's bedroom with overpriced t-shirts strewn about, in what almost appear to be piles of dirty laundry. Three times since 2002, product has been recalled due to protests and boycotts over offensive designs printed on the shirts, making them appear to be more "dangerous" and of course more appealing to the target demographic (dumb teenagers).

Recently, at one nearby location, an actual male model was hired to stand in front of the store wearing nothing but a pair of jeans. Women went nuts getting their photos taken with him. The younger ones were embarrassed and zipped past him on their way into the store, but the truly fascinating thing was how many people walked right by and didn't notice at all.

In what may be one of the most remarkable signs of mass produced global culture exceeding the pace of public standards of decency, police in Virginia Beach seized two store poster displays from an Abercrombie & Fitch in the Lynnhaven Mall, claiming they had received complaints of indecency. The store manager was personally issued a summons for a misdemeanor because the police admitted they had no way to cite the corporate entity directly and how ironic that the manager would likely have been reprimanded by that entity if he hadn't displayed the posters.

If this doesn't alarm you then I don't know what will. Imagine being arrested at work in a clothing store for hanging up a poster. Imagine that if you didn't hang the poster you would be fired. Now imagine that this all took place in an average shopping mall. Can you fault the police? Not really. It's likely that the poster was in fact indecent if it concerned the citizens of that community enough to complain. While I am all for free speech, when these issues come up they usually involve a voluntary act such as the sale of pornographic videos for private home use. In this case, however, the posters were displayed publicly and it is pretty difficult to defend them as legitimate works of art since they were nothing more than advertisements created with the intent to sell products.

Of course the company is responsible and of course it should be held responsible. Some marketing person probably got a raise for creating this controversy and therefore boosting sales. It wouldn't be a surprise to learn that the same marketing person probably called the police multiple times to register the complaints in the first place. When a member of law enforcement is sent to the mall in order to issue a summons to a retail worker in a clothing store for displaying marketing materials, something is horribly wrong with our society. But our laws protect these corporations, and it can be nearly impossible for the average citizen to generate interest by lawmakers to enact such change in the laws. Therefore, as a responsible citizen and consumer you must take matters into your own hands and fight back any way you can. Hint: the best weapon is your wallet.

PROPAGANDER MOUNTAIN

Fashion magazines are one of the key components for disseminating marketing propaganda (because practically any kind of consumer good can be labeled an "accessory"), so let's explore some aspects of marketing and the reality behind them.

Here's a hot new trend: "Denim Bars" that sell jeans or "dungarees," as old people call them, play "hip" music, and serve complimentary alcoholic drinks. At first sight, this wouldn't seem to make any sense until you consider that a mid-range pair of jeans in this kind of store is around $200. Given the price you'd have to be drunk to shop there. For that matter, in case you haven't figured it out by now, any retail environment where you are served complimentary alcoholic beverages (art galleries, auctions, timeshares) should present an enormous red flag that you're most likely about to be ripped off.

"Boutiques" used to offer "hard to find items," but now thanks to the Internet, in the world of mass-produced fashion if anything is hard to find it's because the manufacturer doesn't want it to be found. When a new boutique opens that specializes in "hard to find" items the only thing truly hard to find is the name of the public-relations agent the store hired to get listed in said magazine. I know because I called up several of these stores and obnoxiously asked them how much they paid to be listed in these magazines. At one store I spoke to Nikki, who was not sure, but she said she would check with her boss (also named Nikki) and call me back. The second Nikki called me and gave me the name and number of her publicist, but admitted she got a free quarter-page article about her store in the magazine because she had a friend who worked there.

My favorite one was a boutique in Boston which doubled as a restaurant. If you've eaten at 95 percent of the restaurants in Boston, then no doubt you will see the humor in the fact this establishment has overpriced clothes *and* bad food.

One magazine ran a full-page ensemble replete with a skirt and a pair of pants (in case you need to change outfits in the ladies room while bouncing back and forth between two dates in the same evening). All told, it cost $1288 to piece this stuff together. It takes a lot of balls to suggest that readers blow all that money, especially when you consider a fair share of their editorial staff is apparently from Buffalo.

Without the slightest sense of irony, there is a piece in one magazine about a design which they feel was inspired by the 1930s, the decade in which manufactured consent about the fashion industry came to fruition. Not to be outdone, the next page has an article about fashions inspired by the 1960s, a decade when all of the designers were tripping on acid and it was clearly apparent from their work. Those fashions may have made an impact in 1960, but to the average consumer stoned on Xanax, they just look ugly.

Every five minutes it seems that Native American fashion is back in style, which is hilarious when you consider that modern Native Americans only seem more interested in the White Man's fashion as a way to fleece him in their casinos (note all the name-brand designer stores attached to those casinos). Apparently they're no longer content to sell cheap cigarettes by the side of the road: a pair of designer Native American earrings without any precious metals is $180.

Typical fashion layout pages include photographs of $400 pairs of shoes placed next to photographs of celebrities I don't recognize who are wearing completely different shoes.

There is never any justification for the price of the shoes, such as a pair of flip-flops made by Chanel that cost $345. They are made of PVC, the same plastic used in vinyl siding and plumbing pipes. Why is it used in plumbing pipes? Because it's some of the cheapest plastic in the world, which makes it the most profitable. When I called Chanel's toll-free number (and spoke to another woman named Nikki) to ask why the shoes were so expensive, I was told it had to do with the gas prices and the higher cost of "bringing them over here." You see, this wasn't just any ordinary PVC—it was fine Italian PVC. When I inquired as to the difference in cost between their $345 PVC shoes and the Salvatore Ferragamo PVC shoes also featured on the same page for a mere $150, Nikki told me that it was probably an issue of craftsmanship, that the Chanel shoes were "better-made." At this point, I reminded her that these shoes were simply pieces of molded plastic, but she said this was all the information she had.

On another page of the magazine, an actress with a fake age next to her name is photographed in a t-shirt and jeans, with a jacket over her shoulder. The caption printed next to the photo explains how she likes to keep her look very simple and basic, yet the detailed notes show that she is wearing a $400 jacket, a $300 shirt, $800 boots, and over $13,000 worth of jewelry. You need a magnifying glass to actually see any of the jewelry she is wearing in the photo.

Another actress I have never heard of looks like a team of sadistic hair-stylists attacked her with egg beaters for a week before sticking her finger in an electrical socket. She comments about how the hairstyle makes her look like she isn't trying too hard to be noticed. On the next page, there is another hairstyle that makes her look like a strung-out bag lady; she explains that this hairstyle looks better as the evening continues.

Lindsay Lohan is pictured wearing a pendant around her neck made of 14 karat gold and copper wire, which retails for $999. Rarely do you have the opportunity to honestly suggest that this piece of jewelry may have been purchased at Radio Shack, but there you go. Lindsay Lohan was arrested twice last year for cocaine possession; no doubt the fashion police would have issued an additional citation for this stupid piece of jewelry. You can probably purchase it pre-engraved with the name "Nikki" on the back.

There is a $55 umbrella made out of recycled water bottles which is supposedly owned by two D-list pop stars, a $6600 bracelet worn by a D-list actress, and finally, my favorite, an entire page of expensive makeup featuring an actress talking about how she doesn't like to wear a lot of makeup and prefers to appear "raw."

Sometimes the celebrities featured in these magazines are wholly inappropriate for the items they are promoting. For example, in a recent article, Carrie Underwood, the same person whose music I heard for the first time in a Dollar Tree store, gives tips about how to be "glamorous." Carrie Underwood is about as glamorous as a tow-truck driver.

Anyone dumb enough to follow any of this advice should be smacked upside the head and deported back to West Virginia. Not that there is anything wrong with West Virginia; it's a perfectly good state, it's just not known for its groundbreaking work in the field of fashion.

I love it when the magazines claim to be helping the readers save money, such as a full page ad for a makeup website for which the magazine is co-promoting a 7 percent cashback incentive if you purchase through its affiliate link. Far be it from me to hop on another website only to discover a standard cashback program not affiliated with the magazine is offering 9 percent.

Practically all of the clothes featured in these magazines are referred to as "sexy." What misinformed nonsense. Show any straight man a woman in a $1,000 designer outfit next to her identical twin sister in a $5 pair of spandex shorts and a tight t-shirt with some mildly obscene phrase printed on it, purchased straight from a Rollback rack at Wal-Mart, and ask him which one he thinks is sexier.

One fashion layout extends over a series of two page spreads, the left side reading, "I want" and the right side reading, "I need." The photographs accompanying these taglines show the same outfit adapted for different occasions. All these outfits are well over $1,000 each but, more to the point, the misuse of the word "need" really gets to me. There isn't a person alive who genuinely needs a single thing advertised (and by "advertised," I mean *printed* because, frankly, the editorial content in this waste of a tree is an advertisement for one thing or another) in any of these magazines. All of the wasted ink and paper to promote a meaningless lifestyle that is so far removed from the few legitimate artists who are masters of their craft is disgusting.

Of those masters, among the most intriguing is Georgio Armani, whose company produces cheap knockoffs of their own products and sells them in the mall under the brand "Armani Exchange." In one of the magazines, we see Georgio's daily schedule, which includes a full five hours per day devoted to meals, including a 90-minute breakfast (I'm concerned, do we need to pitch in and buy him dentures?) and it mentions that in the evenings he enjoys karaoke. Women around the world worship clothing designed by a man who essentially has the same schedule as my grandfather does in assisted living.

So after reading all of this meaningless propaganda, I have two serious questions. The first is: what songs does Georgio Armani sing at karaoke? I have tried contacting his public-relations department to find out because I am truly intrigued by this one. You can almost picture him, completely sober, in the back of a cheap sushi restaurant belting out "Paradise by the Dashboard Light" while surrounded by adoring models.

My final question: is everyone who works in the fashion industry named Nikki? Because in calling around to ask questions about what I read, I spoke to more Nikkis in one day than I have ever met in my entire life.

THE ANTIDOTE

Steve & Barry's is a chain which specializes in trying to bring the latest fashions to the consumer at a bargain price. In my opinion, some of their clothes are tacky, such as the leather jackets embroidered with the logos of beer companies; and some are tasteless, such as the t-shirt featuring the gingerbread man from "Candyland," a children's board game which reads "Let's Get Baked!"

My point in including this store is that it has truly brought mass-produced fashion full circle. As of this writing they are selling a "Sex and the City: The Movie" shirt which looks like a bootleg item you might purchase at a flea market. Unquestionably, no character in the "Sex and the City" franchise would be caught dead shopping at a Steve & Barry's, so the fact the merchandise is even sold there should be considered an admission that the lifestyle which is being sold is entirely fictional.

LET US PRAISE THE ALL SMALL
AND MIGHTY DOLLAR

Reach your arms to the sky and scream "Hallelujah!"

Now do it in the middle of a chain clothing store. Take your pick, any clothing store— Gap, American Eagle, Hollister— it doesn't matter. While you're standing there thanking the Good Lord for this bounty of overpriced clothing made by slave labor on a human organ-harvesting farm somewhere in China, I want you to look at the lighting. No, not any kind of divine light from above, but the man-made track or miniature theatrical lighting which is installed in practically all of these stores.

Oh, they use it in other places too, like car dealerships and furniture showrooms, but it's not quite like the lighting in clothing stores. That is because the soft lighting placed in what are known as "hot spots" throughout the store creates visual cues which you subconsciously respond to. It is for this simple reason that the clothes look so much better in the store before you buy, take them home, and think that it's your body which is making them look so drastically different.

Should you go out and blow twenty grand on stage lighting for your bedroom, I can assure you that you will look every bit as spectacular as you thought you would look when you made the purchase in the first place. Far be it from me to tell you that many people try on clothes at home and then return them if they are the wrong size or simply don't like them. Retailers have two answers to this problem: the first is to make the changing rooms "exciting," as if you might pull one of the scantily-clad, near-perfect-looking employees into one of these rooms to make out with. These rooms are decorated to look like some cabana on an exotic island, but in fact the fixtures are made of molded plastic in the same human-organ-harvesting-farms in China by the same slaves who make the clothes. What is the point of this? Well those changing rooms now have the same dramatic lighting as the rest of the store, the better to convince you that the clothes are worth the outrageous prices asked for them.

The other answer to this issue is the returns database. Using a third party provider, you're asked for a drivers license or something similar when returning an item and this information is relayed to a database which checks to see if you're a "frequent returner." If so, the store may refuse to offer you a refund for your purchase by claiming that you could be engaging in fraud. Of course, this is just an excuse to deny your return and keep your money. People who return frequently cost a company money in lost time and unsaleable product, etc. However, these same companies are doing whatever they can to get you to take the product out of the store and are then refusing to take it back once you realize you have been tricked. It's kind of like a game of "Hot Potato," only it could cost you hundreds of dollars when you get stuck holding the potato.

FOURTH MOVEMENT
"CONFESSIONS ON A SALES FLOOR"

FLASHLIGHT IS A VERB

As with any popular song, Parliament Funkadelic's big hit "Flashlight" is often misunderstood. The term "flashlight" is intended as a metaphorical verb, to express the act of "shining a light"on a problem so that people who were "in the dark" about it may be "exposed" to it. Of course, in the case of Parliament Funkadelic, they were once again talking about race relations. I will once again be using it inappropriately to discuss commerce. This is what happens when a majority of your work is abstract; people like me come along and claim it for their own purposes.

The flashlighting was done by one of George Clinton's many characters to one of his other characters who was pretending to be something he was not. By flashlighting him, the character became himself again. This was all played along the lines of black people who pretended to be white people and refused to dance or to allow themselves to have a good time in public for fear of how they would be perceived by whites. By doing so they isolated themselves from other black people, and therefore were not being true to themselves or "the funk."

We need to do a whole lot of flashlighting when it comes to consumerism: think of all the people who think one brand name product trumps another brand name product and who won't want to be seen using one brand name as opposed to another for fear of how they will be perceived by others. We need to flashlight the hell out of people who are embarrassed to use coupons, often because they fear negative comments by cashiers, who insinuate they must be poor if they use them. Why do cashiers do this? Because they don't want to handle the coupons, which take longer for them to settle when they turn in their drawers to the cash room. It's less work for them to insult and humiliate the customer than it is to accept the coupon. We *need* to shine every light we can find on them.

Only by being true to ourselves as people, and demanding that other people be true to themselves will we be able to dance together, and when the whole store is dancing, we will begin to see some positive change.

I HEART LIZ PHAIR

At the age of 17 I became the brutally honest and completely shameless person that I am today. Aside from being beaten into submission in boarding school, I heard a record by Liz Phair called "Exile In Guyville" (a track-by-track response to one of my favorite albums, the Rolling Stones' "Exile on Main Street"). This record really spoke to me in terms of its brutal honesty. It made such an impact on me that every time I question if a situation allows me to be brutally honest or not, I picture the album cover in my head.

So let's be honest.

I have spent the majority of my life broke or in debt.

I spent the majority of my life feeling painfully lonely.

I have always been angered by people I thought were "stupid" or "hypocritical."

I always wanted to be a filmmaker. I never had the money to do it.

I always wanted to be a rock star. I never had the talent to make it.

I know the previous two statements are excuses for my lack of motivation.

I like to play with puppets.

I think I am ugly.

I think I am obese.

Somehow, I still manage to like myself a whole lot.

The point of these statements is not for you to learn about me. It is for you to learn about yourself. Chances are pretty good you identify with one or more of these statements. That in itself is the basis of modern marketing. Modern marketing (which has been around since the 1920's, even though we call it "modern") no longer focuses on how good or bad a product is, but simply which of the above issues a product will eliminate from your life.

THINKING OUTSIDE YOUR PANTS

Once you identify these factors, you can begin to look at a product or service more objectively. I went to a strip club once and it was an awkward experience. The place was so disgusting I didn't want to touch anything or consume anything there. The girls on stage looked so miserable, so bored, so completely out of place. When I left I had a different view of the people who visit these places on a frequent basis. Let's face it, though— most men enjoy strip clubs or they wouldn't be in business. While most men watch pornographic videos, eroticism for me is watching Serena Altschul on CBS Sunday Morning talk about the history of the bikini. While I may be a smaller percentage of the market population, I am reasonably certain there are probably tens of thousands (if not hundreds of thousands) of men who also get an erection every time Serena Altschul is on television. It's just a fact of life.

People react to stimulus. There is certainly a good reason you see so many single women cruising around Home Depot on a Friday night. I used to have a crush on a girl who worked at a candle store, but I never had the nerve to ask her out. When Jean first saw my apartment she asked why I had a collection of fifty or so brand-new scented candles still in the box. I had been there every day after work for months just so I would have a reason to talk to the girl. The store was called Illuminations and they had a mail order catalog as well. Do you know what I did to their market research?

What possible explanation would a computer demonstrate to their marketing department about single men aged 20-25 who purchased an entire scented candle every single day in Northeastern Massachusetts? I'm sure for legal reasons "hot girl at register" was not allowed to appear in a market research report. This is another fundamental problem I have with big box retailers and corporate America in general: it does not allow for human beings to be human beings. Research must be appropriate to be displayed in the corporate environment for which it is intended. Can you imagine a shareholder meeting where someone has to explain "We experienced a sharp increase in retail from the Northeastern division due to a blonde with enormous tits working from 5pm to close"? There's not even a politically correct way to make a statement like that. And just as I am sure other men get turned on by watching Serena Altschul on television, I'm quite certain plenty of other guys probably went into the candle store on a frequent basis and did the same thing.

BIG BOX RETAIL IS RACIST

Big boxes are now trying to segment stores, which means that if they determine from census data that one store is in a "Hispanic" area, the merchandise displayed in the store will be geared toward what the retailer anticipates "Hispanics" want. "Hispanic" is such an awful word. It means Mexicans, Puerto Ricans, Columbians, Dominicans, Guatemalans, Venezuelans, and people from many other countries, people who have nothing at all in common. Many of the racist members in each of these cultures hate each other more than the tens of thousands of men who hate the guy that Serena Altschul is probably at home in bed with right now. They don't want to be grouped together, nor should they be grouped together, as anything other than human beings.

The thing that makes the term racist is that it signifies that you consider a person's background too irrelevant to bother learning what country they're actually from. So how did the term come about? Many people erroneously believe it is derivative of the Latin word "Hispania," when in fact it was a term coined by the US government in the 1970s in order to categorize people for the census. What is the point of categorizing people? Well, that's simple! Good old Edward Bernays, the public-relations guru we discussed earlier, insisted over and over that in order to control crowds they must be categorized as generally as possible. As a country, we are still openly following his playbook to this very day. Some people then try to defend the word "Latino," which actually makes some sense, because it clearly defines a specific place on a map, yet it still suffers from the same problems as "Hispanic." When you generalize people in any form, it is plainly racist (or sexist, or some other kind of "ist"), unless you're talking about executives at Best Buy because they are clearly scum, and after reading this book, I don't think you need to be any particular skin color to realize that.

"Hispanic Hair Care" is an actual divider in some stores, along with "Jewish Foods," and "African American Foods." These are actual signs I have seen in real grocery and big box stores. It's called "segmenting," but I call it "racism." To go on MSNBC and CNN to brag about how you're going to boost profits by "segmenting" stores is outrageous. Yet I have never seen a protest, a boycott, or even an editorial about it. Well, let my voice be heard here and now: it's outrageous, it's insulting, it's disgusting, and shockingly, it appears to be very good for shareholders.

PHYSICAL EDUCATION

As of right now, there are more single than married people in this country. That means more candle stores are having waves of unexplained business than ever before. No, not really, but it does mean that lots of businesses do better thanks to singles. For example, human physical contact is a basic need and desire of all human beings. When you have gone without a hug, a pat on the back, or any physical touch for a long time— and by "long time" I mean weeks or months— then any human contact at all can be overwhelming, even if it is not intended to be.

To that end, I remember getting a haircut once and while the woman was shampooing my hair I remember thinking it was the first time another human being had actually physically touched me in the better part of a few months. That was a really bizarre experience. I found it so disturbing that I never let them shampoo my hair again.

Knowing what I know about people and how they spend money, what with being an economist and all, I wouldn't be surprised at all to learn that that is the reason some people get frequent haircuts.

The same thing could be said of massages, exercise classes, or who knows what else. Wouldn't it be interesting to see the real financial trends there? But again, you're not going to have a meeting at SuperCuts where a pie chart designates "Lonely Perverts" alongside other market segments. But that is what those people would in fact be. This is where mom-and-pop stores need to exist — there is no issue at a mom-and-pop store if you call a customer a "pervert." In a SuperCuts, however, it is probably grounds for termination; now you tell me which is more of a problem?

INTERNET ACCESS

I just went over the list of all my friends to see who I hadn't spoken to in a while and it occurred to me to take a quick survey. Of the 83 names in my phone book, only five people didn't have high speed internet access at home. My 89-year-old grandma has it, which tells you about the five who don't. I will excuse the one who lives in Eastern Canada, and the one in Alaska, because it's cost-prohibitive where they are and the service is of questionable speed.

If you live in the continental United States, however, and you don't have access at home to some form of high speed internet, you're basically enslaving yourself to a broken system that has no choice but to fail you. Without high speed internet it is nearly impossible to live below your means. Some people will say that the monthly expense of $50 is "too expensive"; to them I have to say, you can save at *least* $100 a month by using the internet to comparison-shop everyday items. Surely you can find a way to earn *at least* $100 more a month. And let's not overlook the never-ending free samples, free item coupons, surveys that pay out in gift certificates, and who knows what else?

Sometimes I meet people who have children and refuse to get broadband services in their home. To those of you with children who refuse or don't see the need for these services, I ask why you hate your children so much as to ensure they will be unable to be gainfully employed as adults.

You practically need certification in Microsoft Office just to get a job as a secretary. I have met ten-year-old children who still have no idea how to use an Excel spreadsheet. This is not funny. Yes, some of you are reading this thinking that I'm being an extremist and that I'm out of touch with reality. No, it is YOU who are out of touch with reality. The fact is that there are more of you than there are of me and that's what keeps me up at night. Roughly only 20 percent of the population is online and that is a very scary number. It means 20 percent of the population knows exactly what the other 80 percent are doing and why. It means only 20 percent of the population essentially dictates how the other 80 percent will act, and they plan accordingly.

Your children, as I have already stated, will essentially be enslaved to those of us who are computer literate, since computers already are used to run everything from doctors' offices, highway toll booths, and even McDonald's restaurants. There is a great deal more I have to say about the inability of cashiers to do their job, but it is systemic. If your 16-year-old technophobe applies for their first parttime job flipping burgers, they will quickly find themselves unemployed. The acorn does not fall far from the tree. While you can sit there and say there should be fewer computers, you can't make the technology just disappear. It would be nice to sit at home in your tinfoil hat and wish it all away, but that's not going to help you in the long term, and it is especially detrimental to your children.

Perhaps once upon a time, people figured they would get jobs that didn't require computer use, but every job requires us to use a computer now, from pumping gas to using a microwave oven to working at the post office. Your home telephone most likely has a computer in it. Here's my point: they're everywhere and you use them every day so stop making excuses.

Here's a nice catch-22 for you: I'm often told that people can't afford to buy a computer, but without a computer, it's hard to bargain shop for a computer you can afford. This goes along with my dislike of big box retailers who use lying as a sales technique. If the consumer were just sold the parts they needed, $200 would be more than adequate for the novice to get started online. Computers are sold with so much extra crap and then salespeople try to upsell so heavily that the novice is beyond intimidated and is outpriced immediately.

We once did a whole episode of the show on this topic, but hypocritically, you needed a computer to hear it.

THE GERRIES HIT THE SHOPS

Recently, the big boxes have found their way into the neighborhoods I grew up in and the clash of cultures has been nothing short of hilarious. Millionaires wander through Target assuming all the Chinese-made garbage is of the same fine quality they have always associated with the local merchants. Old people enter Wal-Mart for the first time expecting to be waited on hand and foot. Luddite parents use self-checkout for the first time and don't know how to swipe their own credit cards. Minimum-wage cashiers ask "Credit or Debit?" when customers pay with American Express cards. If you don't know why that last sentence is sad yet funny, please burn this book.

What would make so little sense to either these customers or these employees but is the scary truth is that these Target stores are not entirely Target's core businesses. First and foremost Target owns Target National Bank, which exists solely to issue easy credit for people to spend in their stores. This means that the "target" ('scuse the pun) customer who cannot afford to purchase something in the store will be issued credit at a high interest rate to be paid back to Target itself. I venture to say that on these kinds of sales, Target realizes a far greater profit from the interest on the charge than they do on the profit from the markup on the actual item that was purchased.

Target's second business is even more interesting: forensic investigation services. This business opened its first laboratory in July 2003 and its second in October 2005. Initially opened to cut costs on prosecuting shoplifters and other criminals attempting to defraud Target, it began offering services to local and federal law-enforcement agencies free of charge. This means that while Target didn't make a profit on the work, it was getting tons of experience and data free of charge. These operations still exist today, which is quite terrifying. Target now owns the largest privately owned forensic-services laboratory in the United States.

In what is surely the most alarming aspect of the whole operation, the *Washington Post* reported that Target had given management training to the FBI. This company cannot train their own store managers to sell bars of soap and bottles of shampoo properly and they are offering up help to *law enforcement*?

Yet, as I've said, the customers are too concerned with their own selfish *needs* to contemplate that any of this is even possible, that such a big, clean, friendly store (as they perceive it, it looks like a miserable shithole to me) could ever do anything wrong.

BALDING MAN WITH SCISSORS ON TELEVISION

A lot of finance books and financial advisers tell people to pay for everything in cash. I think this is really awful advice. Paying cash offers you NO recourse if something goes wrong and with the pathetically bad quality of most merchandise, something is almost guaranteed to go wrong. Paying cash offers you no points, miles, or cash back bonuses.

What the financial advisers should be doing is telling people to only charge what they can afford to pay for at the end of the month on a card with a great incentives program and no annual fee, but you almost never hear that. It's just so much easier to show a guy on TV yelling and barking and screaming to "CUT UP ALL YOUR CARDS!! AAAHH THE SKY IS FALLING!! SAVE YOURSELF!!" On paper, though, it is truly terrible financial advice.

Here is some more bad financial advice: paying with a debit card. I scream at the TV every time I hear a financial advisor on a morning show tell people to pay with debit cards. When I see a person pay for something with a debit card I want to rip it out of their hands, use it to slit their wrists, and kick them down a flight of stairs for being so stupid.

Let's pretend you were illiterate, deaf and blind, with no arms or legs, no head, just a torso being wheeled around on a skateboard. The FDIC still requires banks to find some way to communicate with you to explain the fee structure for your bank account, even if it's just "Squeeze the nipple once for yes, twice for no."

What does your fee structure say? It says that when you pay with a debit card and use your pin number that is considered a pin-based transaction, which will be treated like an ATM transaction (hence, when you use your pin number at the supermarket they will offer you cash back), and therefore any fees that apply to using a "foreign" (i.e., a bank other than your own) ATM will apply.

If you use a debit card and pay as a Mastercard or Visa transaction, the merchant is getting hit with standard merchant rates (around 3 percent) and you're not incurring any cost. However, merchants are notoriously unpredictable about how they will process the sale; an authorization can hold the money in your account for ten days or more and you won't have an accurate idea of your balance. That's just fine with your bank because if you screw up and spend too much money (which is not always in your control, as you have no idea what the merchant is doing with your account), they will just hit you with a fee for being overdrawn.

It's usually at this point in the conversation that someone says "but my bank has no fees," and I ask "then how do they stay in business?" Every bank has fees, even if they advertise they have no fees; any "no-fee" deal is almost always for a promotional period of time that may or may not be disclosed in the contract you signed when you opened the account. Go dig those terms and conditions out of the trash and look for the phrase "promotional period"; there will be fees and there will be a lot of them. They are trying to train you not to expect them. Hopefully, you'll just stop reading your bank statement altogether in the future.

Your bank surely supports the balding men on TV when they tell you to pay with a debit card. If you use it as a pin based transaction, they're going to make a dollar or two. If you "wise up" and use it as a Mastercard or Visa swiped transaction, they're going to earn part of the approximately 3 percent fee that the merchant pays, as they are the card issuer. They win either way, you lose either way.

Pay with a credit card, preferably one with a low or no annual fee. Make sure you get rewards points or miles for your purchases. Pay your bill in full every month. Cut the "I can't control myself" or "I'm really bad with money" crap. If you're a grownup, just as with all your other responsibilities, you can control yourself.

BRAND-NAME LOYALTY: A FINANCIAL PLAGUE

Here's another confession: my entire family suffers from a painful and seemingly incurable disease which has never even been defined by any health board and for which there are no statistics as to its effect on the national mortality rate. They suffer from Brand Name Loyalty, or BNL for short. Okay, I'm kidding, but I'm also serious. BNL is a harmless but expensive disease that evinces itself in one relative who will only order office supplies from a company which is routinely six to ten times more expensive than anywhere else, and that's before we talk coupons, rebates, or discounts. This relative does not want "accounts" with anyone else, because they are too overwhelmed to learn how to save money. That's a very common problem which we discussed back at BBY; people get comfortable in how they acquire an item and so come to believe that the cost is irrelevant. Either they priced it out once a long time ago and somehow assumed that this supplier was still the cheapest or they simply become too overwhelmed to find a new supplier.

I have a friend who is on disability and has no other means of earning money. The problem is that by being disabled and by not knowing how marketing works or how to manage his money, he is left constantly bored and broke. Every once in a while when we get a good car-full of free stuff, we go visit him and deliver it all to his apartment. Over time we discovered that after he consumes it all he goes out to the store and, without any coupons or even a sale, purchases the same items at full price because he had discovered he liked them. We were suspiciously becoming viral marketers to people who couldn't afford and didn't need these products but had no other source of learning about them. This is the key: people seem unable or unwilling to discover new sources of product or even new products on their own. This fundamental lack of curiosity seems on paper to have a lot in common with a learning disability of some sort until you realize that the person is perfectly functional in their ability to learn and comprehend, yet somehow when it comes to consumer goods they have programmed themselves to shut off. Perhaps it's just the insane number of choices in the marketplace; down on the corner my local store has over 22 kinds of lottery tickets for sale at any given time. People will tell you they are simply "not interested" but that's not true; it's a function of human nature to want new flavors, new smells, new textures, new colors, new sounds, new stimulus of any kind. Even the most bitter old grouch still has a topic or theme that he still wishes to explore. Either the protocol for getting the thing is too difficult or the choice is too overwhelming.

This is where BNL proves to be such an easy fix for such an easy problem. As I've said, when my disabled friend blows $50 on packaged food he never needed or wanted before, then he doesn't have enough money for his prescriptions or his electric bill.

SUPERSIZE THIS

We all know people who can't tell you where things went wrong, who claim to be victims, who tell you the price of everything makes it impossible to live on such and such amount (and in some cases it truly is). An excellent example of the sort of hypocritical or uneducated myth here would be in an episode of "Thirty Days" by Morgan Spurlock, in which he and his partner try to live on minimum wage for 30 days and are unable to make ends meet.

There were two key scenes in this show that really bugged me and that I have not heard addressed anywhere. The first was the grocery shopping. I froze the frame on the cash register total and saw they used NO coupons at ALL. Considering they were eating strictly vegetarian it should have been dirt cheap for them to eat for a month with just the standard produce deals and canned / frozen vegetable deals that run constantly. I understand that he was trying to prove that the minimum wage is way too low, and it is, but in my view what he ended up demonstrating was this idea of stretching a dollar the only way he knew how. I never once saw them go to the public library and pick up a book about how to save money or use a free computer at the library to learn about coupons or rebates online and print them out for free.

While they were very crafty about various ways to save money on certain things, they never touched on stores like Rent-A-Center which are so harmful to people on low wages who need expensive items and don't know how to get them.

Just as you never see a Panera Bread in a bad neighborhood, you never see a Rent-A-Center in a good neighborhood. There was no discussion of that and it upset me because it didn't paint a clear picture of the people trying to take advantage of the disadvantaged other than the hospitals he visited.

In one scene his girlfriend needs a prescription, so they go to a chain drugstore to fill it and they don't use a coupon for a free gift card when you fill a new prescription. Those gift cards are $10 at Target and usually $25 everywhere else. For a couple who was sharing a bus pass, they could have eaten frozen and canned goods for at least another week with that gift card. There was a lot of scrimping but no saving. It was a disappointment.

I am probably so angry about that episode because I have made all those mistakes for most of my life as well. My first jobs were all minimum wage until I started to exploit my knowledge of computers. Many of the job listings in the *Village Voice* when I was a teenager were all sorts of scams which tried to make money off desperate people looking for employment.

When I got my first credit card, I fell into the same trap that most teenagers fall into now— the idea that it's "free money" or that somehow I would only have to pay a few dollars a month minimum payment for the rest of my life. When I was 18 I had perfect credit and a good savings account; by my 19th birthday I was a good $10,000 in debt, all my cards were cancelled, and I had no savings left.

None of this stopped me from spending every last dollar I made as soon as it was in my hands. Often Friday's paycheck would be gone by Sunday afternoon and I would scrape through the week "saving money" by doing ridiculous things like eating every meal from the 99-cent menu at McDonald's. I was physically hurting myself, emotionally hurting myself, and financially hurting myself for no good reason other than I apparently had some need to be miserable at that time in my life.

Somehow I was happy to be out making a living and spending it on useless garbage, yet was miserable at how much I was hurting myself by doing so. I couldn't figure out how this cycle had begun or how it would end and it bothered me a great deal.

One of the things I remember was how nice it was to eat in a restaurant, no matter how awful. Even though I was very shy and did not speak to anyone, and even though the food was never really all that good, somehow it seemed much nicer and less lonely than eating at home by myself. Whenever we go out to eat these days I still pay careful attention to the people I see eating alone, because there is something just bizarre about the whole ritual. I could never really afford to spend $30 a night on dinner; more than half my paycheck was going to dinners at one point in my life, and these were the kind of casual dining meals I have discussed earlier, almost all of which made me physically ill afterward.

When I said that there's basically an embarrassment tax in this country, that's because I've paid it plenty of times myself. Heck, I'm only writing this book in the hope that maybe ONE person reads it and won't have to hit bottom before they change. That would be a tremendous success to me.

On multiple levels, it's completely disgusting that at 22 with over $20,000 worth of education, the average college graduate finally discovers that all the same chain stores they grew up with were not truly unique to their hometown and in fact cover the entire landscape of North America.

This was not my problem, though; no, mine was much more serious. I ironically and passionately embraced the fact that there was so much of the same. I would do road trips such as trying to visit every Blockbuster video in one state, then every Firestone Tire in the next. If the brands wanted to be treated as true public institutions, who was I to argue? Some people collect kitchen magnets from the places they've been; I collect store-brand merchandise from each grocery chain I visit, along with an enormous keychain of affinity cards like some perverse sort of consumer passport showing all the places I've been. I collected bottled iced tea and got one bottle of every new brand I found around the country, at one point filling three bookshelves in my living room. Once I filled the entire car with potato chips, with no two bags of the same brand or flavor. The collection lived in my parents garage until it was eaten by mice.

Fully embracing consumerism and artificial culture in a celebratory and shameless way was an interesting experience as well. You can become so comfortable, so overly indulged, that you end up living in a coma-like state of constant bliss. Since you no longer expect any quality or service and you no longer care about cost or delay, everything is always perfect. All the artificial holidays become true causes for celebration, each requiring its own expensive ritual. Even my shoes needed to be more comfortable because my regular sneakers were interfering with my peace of mind. Everything was someone else's fault, nothing was my problem; if I encountered a problem I simply handed over my credit card and my problem went away. Who needed prescription drugs to feel nothing? When you're extremely comfortable all the time you really don't feel anything.

Sounds like a commercial for a Sport Utility Vehicle, right?

Sadly, we all seem to go through a phase like this for a short time, and while most of us get over it, so many people of all ages decide it's how they want to live and continue to do so.

Here's the big-box consumer's mantra:

"Nothing is my fault. Nothing is my problem. If there is a problem, I'll hand over my credit card and it will go away."

Want to know when reality strikes? Most of you already know it's the moment your credit card is declined, but people are still learning that every day. Like I said, it's usually temporary because that's when you've maxed out your card. But this blissful feeling can certainly be very addictive and that's what the retailers and issuing banks are counting on.

Do you really want to save money? I mean, really truly want to save money? It's so simple: you need to be honest with yourself, you need to be honest with those around you, you need to be honest with the retailers, and you need to be honest with the card issuer.

When Jean or I are running low on money, we discuss it so that neither one of us will request or expect anything out of the ordinary. So many men I know feel like their wives or girlfriends require expensive gifts on a regular basis and feel they won't be "loved" if they do not deliver; this pressure makes them act out in a variety of other ways. Everyone wants to feel loved and cared for, but money should have nothing to do with it. If you're making bad financial choices, your spouse has every right to be mad at you, but putting a dollar amount on your emotions is absolutely crazy in any situation. If your emotions tell you that your spouse's regard for you is tied to your financial contribution, go price-match a hooker. They're in business because they're cheaper than spouses who may demand financial compensation for your perception of love and / or sex acts. By the same token, if your emotions tell you that you *have* to purchase an item but you can't explain why, go put the money towards a therapist; it's much better spent that way.

My friend Alex tells a great story about waiting in line for hours at the first McDonald's in St. Petersburg and a number of the Russians who had spent a week's salary on hamburgers and fries spitting them out in disgust. It's basically the same story.

I thought the first Kmart in New York City was hilarious. Half the merchandise was locked up in glass cases so no one could shoplift it, but there were very few sales people to open the cases to get the merchandise out. They are still in business, which is a total shock to me, but also a testament to how low the standards of retail have fallen here as more and more people move to New York and think that this is the "way things are done."

SYOSSET

Waldbaum's is a grocery chain which specializes in two things: grocery stores disguised as homeless shelters and luxury resorts disguised as grocery stores. There are no happy mediums in the chain; either the location looks like it should be fire-bombed or it looks like a palace. We stick to the ones that look like palaces (and have a concierge desk).

One of the great joys of shopping at certain Waldbaum's is self-checkout. I can listen to the Rolling Stones on my iPod, run my own merchandise, and avoid a semantics argument with a cashier. But then we encountered something we never expected, which surely would only exist in such a rural store in an urban environment. The immigrant who thinks the chain store is a good, well-meaning employer, who therefore seeks to do everything for the good of the company, as if it were the '50s and he was working for General Motors as an engineer. The employee who thinks that if he needs a gall bladder operation the "owner" will give him paid time off or appreciate that he is doing a good job or any of the other antiquated bullshit that existed before you had to get a credit check and drug test just to get a job pumping gas.

His name was Jawn, pronounced just like "John," a name he clearly picked so he could sound more American without having to spell out letters in Click every time he was asked how to pronounce his name. The fact that such a large chain hired a man who proudly couldn't spell a four-letter word is evocative of the source of the problem itself. And things would only get worse as I tried to use a coupon on which the terms and conditions were written in tiny little letters.

Now I have my fair share of experience dealing with cashiers who pretend not to speak English. My favorite is Patti; after denying Jean the use of some coupons, a week later she tried to tell me that the coupon I presented her with was "too confusing" and therefore she wouldn't take it. But wouldn't you know, I was prepared and handed her the exact same coupon printed in Spanish from the previous week's "El Diario" and said "there, is that one easier for you?" The look was priceless, and so was the lesson; she never argued with me again.

Back to Jawn at Waldbaum's. Aluminum foil was on sale 10 for $10, and a 50-cents off one coupon was attached to the package, which doubled, thereby making the foil free. Halfway through ringing them up, the screen froze, and Jawn strolled over. "No you can't use this one!" he shouted over "Exile on Main Street."

There should be a law about shouting over that record unless it's a medical emergency.

He told me that I couldn't get the aluminum foil for free as, "it would be stealing. You will cost Waldbaum money!" I did my usual "Waldbaum? Just the one? They wouldn't both lose money?" to which I got the look of "how dare you correct my broken-ass English!"

He had committed the ultimate sin of interrupting my music and dragging my checkout time to a screeching halt, so he was about to get it. "First of all, dipshit, the *manufacturer* pays the company the 50 cents. Secondly, I'm sorry the coupon says "Do Not Double" and your shitty cash register doubled it anyway; maybe if the board of directors coughed up ten grand for some halfway decent POS software you wouldn't be having this problem now. But no, you're gonna sit there for $8 an hour and daydream about how the 'owner' is going to take care of you for doing a good job. There is no 'owner' stupid, there are shareholders and they don't give a fuck how many coupons I use as long as the sales totals are high at the end of the day so their shares go up on the market. Do you even know what the market is? Do you think anyone at this company gives a flying fuck about you or your voyage by boat from whatever third world country you crawled out of to come here and do the job a teenager should be doing? Now leave me the fuck alone so I can get my free aluminum foil, which I will donate to charity since I already have a closet full of it."

There was a long pause. Other customers were looking. Jean had long since run away so as to not be seen with me. The other cashiers were glaring at me and Jawn looked around in horror at them. Finally came the reply, "who tell him how much money I am making? This is not right!"

I said, "go shove the aluminum foil up your ass! And give me my coupons back!" and walked out calmly. Then I went to the Dunkin Donuts next door and sat down with a coffee. About ten minutes later I saw Jawn go outside for a cigarette, so I ran back in the store and bought up *all* the foil. I didn't even want it, I just wanted to prove a point. By the time he got back to his post, I had used all four self-checkouts simultaneously and filled a shopping cart with the foil. I had receipts to prove I had "paid" for them, even though they were all free. I tossed Jawn a box and said "eat those and shut up."

After I packed them all in the trunk of the car, I went back into the store with my empty cart. I had scored the aluminum foil, but I still had to do the deal on Pop Tarts.

Now at this point you're thinking, "What a racist this guy is! What about understanding people from different cultures!" You couldn't be more wrong. The point is that he interrupted "Exile on Main Street" for no reason other than his own stupidity. Wasting my time is unacceptable. I had to take the time to get the coupons, figure out the deal, drive to the store, and then drive the foil them to the soup kitchen. I mean, why is it okay for him to interrupt me, essentially call me a thief, and then make up some non-existent rules in order to protect his fantasy of some "employer" that he doesn't really have? It's not. And if he had been black, white, brown, yellow, green, red, or purple I would have treated him just the same. I believe all sexes, races, creeds, and colors are equally deserving of my harassment when they start to try to force their own made-up beliefs on me. The exception to this is if you're in their place of residence or worship. I mean, you don't walk into a church and then get offended if someone tries to convert you. But that wasn't the case here. I was in a grocery store, not a church. We live in a capitalist society and Jawn doesn't get that yet.

FAIRNESS

Another fundamental problem is the concept of what is "fair"; it's this idea of what is fair based on the pretense of your culture. In a small village where a tribe of people sleep in huts and tents the word "fair" means something very different from what it means in Chicago, Los Angeles, or New York.

I get this a lot on "Coupon Queen" message boards, where people have a bunch of coupons but only take some of the merchandise and leave the rest for other shoppers because that's what is "fair." Here's fair: you and I make a deal and we both honor our ends of it, that is fair. If I go in a store with a hundred coupons and they only have 50 of the products, I'm taking all 50. I don't care if you get any. If you get there before me, take them all, they're all yours, and it's fair because you got there first. If I see you in the parking lot and you tell me you really need a couple, they're all yours, help yourself, I'm not a jerk. But don't start up with this "fair" garbage. Grow up! "Fair" is a word for children with rich parents. Yes, I often lose out to things that are not fair, we all do. To people who tell me it's not fair that I take all the free merchandise I can get, I say, get over it, get over yourself, and while you're busy doing that you just missed out on all the cereal; better hurry up before I get all the tampons and cat food!

Jawn and people like him try to impose the idea of "fair" that they take from somewhere very far away and apply it to my aluminum foil and raisins. The whole concept is so foreign to him, you're half-worried he'll try to ritually execute you in the seafood department, and you can't entirely fault him for that. The problem here is he clearly does not belong in the customer service industry. Should he find employment here? Absolutely. Should he be properly compensated for his labor and be afforded the same legal protections as any other legal alien working towards his citizenship? Absolutely. What if he's a hard worker and ends up getting his brother a job at the store? Why not? Seems like a good idea to me! Should either of them be in customer service or work as cashiers until they have clearly done a better job of assimilating into our culture? Not a chance in hell. It's just like the problem of having mentally retarded baggers—who is left to deal with the problem? The customer, who else?

CHARITABLE CAUSES

I have another confession: I did something really bad. Actually, I still do it every year around Thanksgiving. I can't help myself. You know at the grocery store how they have the bags of food to donate to the homeless and hungry? It's a pretty typical setup: at the entrance to the store there are brown paper bags which are stapled shut. Inside each one are some canned and boxed items. You take the bag to the register and pay a fixed price (usually around $10) and then place the bag in a large collection box near the exit. After a few weeks, just before the holidays, the store donates the box to a local charity to be disbursed to the hungry in your community. For years I always bought multiple bags. Having been homeless twice, I am always looking for ways to help out, because being homeless is one of the worst feelings in the world. Anything I can do to help someone out in that situation I am only too happy to do.

What do I have to confess? One year after we started couponing I actually opened one of the bags to see what was in it. Three dollars worth of merchandise, pre-discount. That means that if I had bought these same items with coupons I could have gotten them for less than twenty-five cents. The store claimed these items were a pre-determined selection of the most needed items, but I didn't believe that. The bags contained the sort of items the store couldn't get rid of, and here they were selling them at a crazy markup, so it appeared that the products were now flying off the shelves. I asked the store manager if they donated any of the money from the bags that were sold and he said he didn't think so; just the food itself. I inquired to the store via mail and email but, not surprisingly, never got a response.

Sure, this was just one chain, but as we traveled that year I discovered this was a pretty common practice all over the country. Now this store was the same store Jawn and his brother worked in where they were "defending" who-knows-what by giving me a hassle and not accepting my coupons. Trying to explain this to them would be like talking to a brick wall, since they refuse to believe anything bad could possibly happen in such a "clean and modern" store. You know who else thinks things like that? Children. The same ones who believe things should be fair.

I don't want to discourage anyone from donating to charity. If a food drive is going on please donate; everyone needs to help each other out, probably most of all *because* life is not fair, but this doesn't mean that the store should profit further from your donations. Just because there's a food drive doesn't mean you should suddenly be guilted into paying $3 for a can of soup. Use your coupons and rebates, get the same discount you would get for yourself, and then donate as much as you can to the charity. If you don't have coupons or discounts, just give them *cash* and let them decide how to spend it. We can all hope they will spend it properly, but there are no promises. Most charities are so focused on doing the job of helping the people they are set up to help that they become "top heavy," which means they have too much overhead and most of your money ends up going to the work of running the charity as opposed to aiding those you are trying to help.

For a long time I tried giving money directly to people in need; specifically, in our neighborhood we only have one panhandler and over the course of a year I had given him over $500. I often sat down with him to discuss his situation and see if there was any way I could help him other than money; clearly the cash wasn't doing him too much good, since he was still homeless. After a while it became pretty clear that he was mentally ill and was refusing treatment, which was his right. This was a difficult situation and an ugly situation, and, let's face it, it's one that most people don't want to deal with. It's a lot easier just to pay ten bucks for a sealed paper bag in the supermarket and walk away feeling good. But homelessness, hunger, and mental health are really, really big and important issues which aren't just solved with food drives. The idea that these stores you can supposedly trust go so far as to attempt to profit from the confusion and lack of balls required to solve the problem is outrageous. Yet I have never seen a protest outside a grocery store unless there were wages involved. This fascinates me to no end.

Maybe that's because people are shopping for dreams, not products. It's not my place to argue the actual quality of the goods and services; *Consumer Reports* does a much better job of that than I ever could. So it's no wonder that paying the ten bucks, feeling good, and walking away is such a popular option at Thanksgiving. Where else do we see this concept of buying merchandise at a poor value to alter our moods?

"FEELING A" IS SHOPPING

Travel agencies are usually a good place to start, since running away from your problems is a popular way to avoid dealing with them. Take it from an expert who saw the Rolling Stones 40 times on the *Forty Licks* tour—I was running away from a whole lot of problems at home. The idea sold to every Stones fan that "this may be your last chance to ever see them," has been milked to such an extent that it has become more of a punchline than a mantra, and yet it still works over and over again. One of the most classic small town travel agency rackets is the poster in the window for an all-inclusive tropical resort vacation with women in bikinis (no, not Serena Altschul, trust me, I've checked several times). The racket works like this: guy passes travel agency on his way to bank/post office/coffee shop every morning, sees hot girl on poster with her boobs hanging out. So one day he walks in and is told he can "affordably" take this vacation for one "low price" and since it's "all-inclusive" he won't have to worry about what everything will cost when he gets there. The travel agency gets him with the following hook: "Don't you deserve to do this just once in life? You're wasting away at that factory, that's not why you were put on this planet, you need to be out there living your life!"

Our friend Marbles brilliantly notes that no personal accomplishment in life is so belittled and meaningless than it is seen in the context of an office party to celebrate the event with a bunch of people whose personal lives you know nothing about. No true defining moment of your life should ever take place at an "all-inclusive" resort unless pregnancy or death are involved.

Worker guy makes a layaway-style deal with the travel agent. Every Friday after he cashes his check he stops by to make a payment, until after a couple of months he is booked and ready to go. When he arrives at the resort, he discovers that while everything is "all inclusive" they're usually out of everything and instead of meeting lots of hot girls like the one on the poster he is now standing on a beach with hundreds of other men looking around to see where the hot girls are. He then spends the next six days drinking Budweiser, jerking off, and watching sports on television. Pretty much the same as his recreational activities at home.

I've met grown men who still believe the carnival midway banter they heard at an all-inclusive resort fifteen years ago and they can still quote every word. "They had the single most expensive cuts of meat; these were world-class famous chefs from the finest restaurants who worked there for free in exchange for the free vacations." They still cling to the various premiums they purchased at the gift shop. Meanwhile, their kids have seen three-quarters of the country by car as they follow Pearl Jam around. Then the parents tell you that the kids "lack direction." I think their direction is pretty clear—as far away from that small town as possible (it's the ones who stay that scare them).

The kids are shopping for dreams too—the dream of escaping the reality of living in that small town, and that dream can cost them just as much. Like I said previously, the credit card offers give them a false sense of security and they may try to buy their way out of town with money they don't have, only to arrive in their new home with nothing except a mountain of debt and few real skills. If you're looking for proof of this phenomenon, they all hang out in student ghettos like Allston, Massachusetts and Brooklyn, New York. You hear about how great these places are because old people like to make themselves feel young by visiting these neighborhoods, sitting in street cafés, and watching young people act overly dramatic and enthused about everything from lighting fixtures to carrot sticks. The oldsters keep muttering things like, "remember when we were that age?" but there's nothing really great about any of it. Then they drive back home at night, never permanently migrating, because deep down they know these student ghettos are the result of massive failure. The kids all blog about how great their lives are, but when your life is truly great you don't have time to wipe your ass, let alone write about it. Take it from someone who's done quite a bit of blogging when the Stones were not on tour.

ONE TICKET TO PARADISE

Most of all, compulsive gamblers shop for dreams and since there's a lottery machine in every grocery store, I get to meet a lot of compulsive gamblers. My favorite are the scratch-ticket junkies because they are so desperate for a win that their behavior can modify itself in interesting ways. Once a year one of our local stores issues these scratch tickets for charity. The ticket costs $1 and has two parts: on the first part you have to match three like amounts to win that amount as a cash prize. On the second part each ticket has a coupon for one free product and the ticket you get determines the product you get.

These coupons are among the most valuable all year because they are store coupons for free, so you can still use a manufacturer's coupon in conjunction with the store coupon and get overage. Technically, the store is paying you the overage, not the manufacturer, and since they are too cheap to update their POS software or roll out the promotion properly their loss is your gain. Anyway, these tickets go on sale and the store manager stands at the front of the store with a microphone and advertises these scratch tickets all day long (all grocery store managers are frustrated they didn't make it as disc jockeys) and then they run deals like free donuts and coffee when you buy ten tickets.

The gamblers just care about the money, so they throw out the free product coupons. You can just hang out and they'll give you all the free product coupons you want. I usually buy about $50 worth of the tickets to start with, since it is for charity and that is the primary thing to remember before taking advantage of the rest of the promotion. Most people buy one or two at the register on their way home and never look at them again. Here's the thing I find really interesting: if you go through the aisles and sometimes to multiple stores in the chain, a good number of the "free" items aren't sold or even made in the size specified. Now I will say that the store managers are usually decent people who allow you to substitute for similar items and they do make good on their promises, but it would be considerably cheaper for the store to just print tickets for goods that are actually available at the store.

Part of this may be a problem in regional distribution; there are so many stores in so many states that some of the items are only available in one state and not in another, but why is that the customer's problem? Why should the customer have to care about the store's inability to run its operation? When the cashier can't figure out how to use the register and so he just makes up arbitrary rules about whether you can use a certain coupon, instead of admitting he doesn't know how to ring it up, how is that the customer's problem? If he requests help and you stand there for 30 minutes waiting for four people to figure out how to ring up the coupon, why aren't you compensated for your time? Aren't you essentially working for the store as a consultant in the capacity of cashier training at that point? Why is it the customer's problem? When you call a customer service number for help, why do they issue you a "case number"? If you pick up an item and put it down somewhere else, why do the employees give you a look because you're making more work for them? *They work there! That is what they are paid to do—work!* Nothing pisses me off more than when an employee says, "Let me help you out with that" in a condescending tone as if they are doing you a huge favor. Customer service means just that—the employee is there to service the customer.

BADLANDS

At this very moment in the United States there are over 100 "mixed use" shopping centers in operation. This is something that makes environmentalists rather happy. A mixed use center is one in which retail and residences reside on the same property, eliminating the need to waste fuel on transportation. But how many environmentalists have really thought about mixed use and what it means to the consumer? How many have considered what it means to the community or to the culture?

These shopping centers open and the locals are thrilled that they have a new place to visit. The design is usually the same: instead of an indoor mall or a strip mall, a "streetscape" is built, which attempts to replicate the facade of a downtown street in any small town in America during the 1950s. The visual cues make people feel more comfortable shopping than they would in a standard shopping mall. Bed Bath and Beyond ends up looking like a friendly local merchant as opposed to the mass merchant retailer that it is.

Gradually, medical offices begin to open on the property, as do residences, and then parking and traffic are a problem. It occurs to the residents that there are no supermarkets, and if there are they are rather overpriced. It turns out that there is very little competition of any kind in the entire shopping center, which essentially fixes the price of certain items. The children growing up in these residences have nowhere to play and spend a majority of their time hanging out in retail environments. It's not hard to guess what happens next. As soon as there is any kind of problem with the water or the electricity or any other community issue, the residents realize that they have no government to complain to.

That's because the entire new fake city which has emerged at the blessing of the environmentalists (who may have opposed it otherwise) is built on unincorporated territory, thus making the property management company by default the judge and jury in any kind of dispute. Sure, there are state laws which need to be followed, perhaps even county laws, but, generally speaking, the management company is free to do whatever it wishes. The residents find themselves practically enslaved, living, working, eating, and eventually dying in what is nothing more than a shopping mall.

"The Village at Sandhill" in South Carolina is one such place, and it looks more like "The Village" from the television show "The Prisoner" than it resembles a nice, quiet place to live. The property boasts twelve women's clothing stores, fourteen restaurants, two Starbucks Coffee stores, one supermarket, and a whole lot of ignorant people supporting the complex with their hard-earned money. I pulled in to use the restroom and I drove away as quickly as I could, screaming my head off about what a living nightmare it was.

In order to build one of these monstrosities you need three things: money; a large plot of unincorporated land; and steady numbers of people that you think will be dumb enough to fall for it.

I have nothing at all against the state of South Carolina, but based on the scope of this property alone it is clear how marketers and developers perceive you. Like I said, we now have over a *hundred* of these faux-cities operating in the United States. If you live near one, now may be the time to move.

ANOTHER BIG SECRET

Generally speaking, chain store retailers do not have a contingency plan for when a customer demonstrates common sense. One of my favorite examples of this occurred at a Walgreens store in Florida on the evening of January 1, 2007 An unknown woman got into an argument with a cashier. Dissatisfied with the outcome of the argument, she slowly walked through the store aisle by aisle and proceeded to light merchandise on fire with her cigarette, attempting to burn the store to the ground. The store quickly filled with smoke and the customers and staff were evacuated. This story was reported nationally in the news the following morning, but was never truly investigated by any of the news media.

Let's look at this story a little more closely. The cashier has thus far been unable to provide a complete picture of the argument. The press reported that the argument was over the amount of change the woman was due "or something." Then you have the issue that not a single member of the staff noticed a customer smoking inside the store, compounded by the really astounding fact that none of them noticed her methodically lighting merchandise on fire aisle by aisle. Nor did they even notice the store was on fire for quite some time, as smoke began to billow out of the aisles before anyone noticed any of this was going on. The woman remains unnamed because after lighting the store on fire, she simply walked away, never to be found or identified.

What makes this story even more remarkable? At least a year later, the store manager (the aptly named Mr. Forest) is still employed by Walgreens! When I called him to inquire about the events of that day, he had no comment except to say that he was not on duty the day that the event transpired.

But as a manager, certainly he would have supervised and trained the staff who were so completely inept at preventing such a rational response to their own apathy. I am not supporting arson, but it makes perfectly good sense that if you piss off enough customers and don't care about your job, sooner or later one of them is probably going to try to burn down the store. Anyone with half a brain for retail would know that, but you don't need half a brain for retail to work at a Walgreens, you just need a pulse. Some days, even that would appear to be questionable.

OBITUARY

The artificial notion that a big box retail store is a community that cares about its environment, employees, and surrounding community is just that—artificial. The store has one legal responsibility and that is to its shareholders. It's practically illegal for them to put the employees' needs above the shareholders or the customers' needs over that of those shareholders. And this is precisely why I could give a crap about the big box retailers or their employees. I am a nice, friendly, caring person, but when you enter a store you're entering a business environment in which, regardless of all the superficial bullshit, you're there to conduct business, as are the employees. Yes, I hang out like it's a bar, yes, I try to enjoy myself by listening to music and browsing the merchandise, but when it comes to the register I take a sixteen-cent sale as seriously as most people take buying a home—because it's my money, not the employee's. The employee who is too lazy to resolve a coupon dispute is trying to tell me how to spend my money, and who are they to have the right to do so? When they roll their eyes over a forty-cent coupon, I have to ask them "may I have forty cents?" because it's my money, not yours, so don't tell me how to spend it. Occasionally, they do give me the forty cents and toss the coupon. After they are done ringing me up, I don't say thank you; instead I remind them, "That's why you're still working here, because you don't care about how you spend your money."

The average Rolling Stones concert ticket is $350. Earlier I confessed to being a hypocrite sometimes and this is a perfect example. But it makes me who I am as a consumer. I don't blink at the Stones tickets, but I will flip out over a twenty-five cent mistake at the register. If Keith Richards were the cashier, however, I wouldn't care at all about the twenty-five cents.

I also get really angry knowing that I am supporting a business that pays the cashiers so little and ends up with a lot of bad labor as a result. When I worked in stores, I took the money very seriously because, after all, money is why you're in business. You would think that you'd want the best and brightest labor you could get to handle the most important part of the store—the money—but instead it's often the smartest and most technologically savvy people who work at the loading dock and deal with all the paperwork.

So I'm pleased to get as much from the store at the smallest cost. I couldn't care less about creating more work for them, since they couldn't care less about creating more work for me. You have to behave a bit like a bull in a china shop in big boxes because they treat you like garbage. The only reason you exist is to give them your money, to fall for their marketing, to consume, to spend, and to come back tomorrow and do it again. Our feelings of helplessness, of despair at the state of the human race, and of discouragement when we look at these monolithic warehouses of mass-produced crap are all based on preconceived notions about the role of the consumer. People who attempt to "fight back" by only shopping at local, independently owned stores are misguided; you fight back by getting the stores to pay for your merchandise, by getting manufacturers to pay the stores for your merchandise, by getting banks to pay the stores for your merchandise, and you do it all legally and legitimately with various coupons, promotions, and rebates. By using the tools with which you are presented, it's entirely possible to do, and I personally have done it, so I believe it strongly.

How do you know you're winning when you are fighting back? You never take cash out of your pocket, or only in very minimal amounts. If you walk out of a store with $200 worth of merchandise and you have only paid $3 or $4, you're winning. At that point, it doesn't matter whether it was the merchant, the manufacturer, or a bank who paid for your goods; all that matters is that you didn't pay, and that you broke the mold of the consumer. I am not an environmentalist, so I can't tell you about the impact of your purchase, but I can tell you about the financial portion.

Don't think the stores won't try to fight back. Best Buy has already started with their "angel" and "devil" customer profiling, not to mention their intention to stop issuing mail in rebates ("as a convenience to the consumer"), which means they plan to charge full price for everything instead of making discounts available.

Don't think the people trying to fight back by purchasing elsewhere are winning either. Recently at a second-hand shop I saw $1 Wal-Mart DVDs priced at $5, and I overheard a customer saying, "you can't shop at *new* merchandise stores anymore, they're just too expensive!"

Ten years ago I was in a gas station in South Carolina with my friend Scott. He put a Coke and some Pop Rocks on the counter and the cashier refused to sell it to him. This woman in her mid-fifties had heard eating the Pop Rocks and drinking the Coke would make you explode and she believed it.

We thought she was kidding, but she was very serious. She absolutely refused to sell it to him. So we threw $5 onto the counter, walked away, and he ate the Pop Rocks and swallowed some Coke at the other end of the store while she was *freaking out* behind the counter and calling 9-1-1. We got the hell out of there before the police showed up because we didn't want to spend all night trying to explain this one with out-of-state plates. But I still remember it vividly and it's all I can think of whenever a cashier starts trying to put her personal beliefs over the sale. If you can't endorse what you're selling, go work somewhere else, no one is forcing you to work at that store. Scenes like this evoke the mistaken notion people have that retailers are public institutions for the good of the community.

I mean, can you imagine standing in a store where an employee is telling you that you *don't* want to buy a product there because it interferes with her own beliefs? What? They've just sold a customer a $30 extended warranty on a $20 item and told him it was a "great deal," but suddenly they're taken by a need to be honest and they want to avoid selling a product? It's like a Monty Python sketch come to life. I expected John Cleese to appear any moment wearing a rubber chicken on his head.

This is the essence of "Retail Anarchy"—absolutely no one is in charge. There is no real order. As much as retailers and manufacturers want to believe there is, they're wrong. They're so bad at rolling out anything, human nature is so unpredictable, and people are so different on a cultural level that it's clear the big box retailer is a complete failure.

THE FRANCHISEE, THE DUMBEST CUSTOMER OF THEM ALL

In a Boston Market I ordered a soup and sandwich combo only to discover that the soup they gave me was a small order, not the medium-sized listed on the menu. After much bickering, the employee told me that they no longer stock the medium-sized cups and "I don't know why they put that up there." For a full ten minutes we argued about the size of the soup, as a long line of miserable people formed behind me. Finally, she gave in and took a large soup cup and filled it twice with small soup cups, as if the two inches of soup were coming out of her paycheck. She had no idea that in 1997 Boston Chicken (Boston Market's former name) settled a $19 million class action brought by its very own investors for publishing misleading statements in its financial reports. She had no idea that Boston Market has more to do with real estate than it does to do with serving chicken dinners. Most of all, she had no idea that I had a cold and my patience with her nonsense was running very thin.

A Burger King franchise owner has sued the Burger King corporation for requiring them to offer items on the "Dollar Menu" when their stores were located in high rent areas of Manhattan. The franchisee claims that it would be impossible to stay in business (and they did go out of business) if they were required to sell hamburgers for $1. Nobody thought to ask the franchisee why he felt that anyone who lived or worked in an area with such high rents would ever want to eat at Burger King.

C-Town, a cooperative of individually owned and operated supermarkets, was advertising ground beef at some cheap price. My friend Alex went there every day for five days trying to purchase it, but each day was told that it would be in stock tomorrow or that the butcher was on vacation, or some other excuse. On the final day of the sale, he demanded to speak with the store manager who ended up literally on his knees and in tears, declaring "I just can't afford to sell the things at the prices C-Town makes us advertise them at!"

Franchise owners always boast about what entrepreneurs they are, which is in direct contrast to the relatively high rate of failure experienced by new franchise openings. I have personally read franchise opportunities that any 12-year-old with a calculator could tell you were practically designed to fail, thus putting more money in the hands of the franchiser in the form of fees and materials. It is clear too that franchising is for people without an original idea or an original product or service to offer.

From this we can determine that it is the franchisee who is truly the worst customer of them all, shelling out tens of thousands of dollars with dreams of becoming rich by selling mass-produced garbage in volume on a low markup. Once upon a time this may have worked, but since you can barely spit these days without hitting a retailer selling mass-produced garbage in volume on a low markup, the competition almost instantly negates any potential for profit.

IF IT'S ALL MASS-PRODUCED CRAP, WHY IS IT SO EXPENSIVE?

The easiest way to make money is by saving money. So if you're trying to maximize profits, it makes sense to save money any way you can. Now let's look at what you will charge. Let's say that you run a hotel with ten rooms and you're charging $100 per night. If the hotel is full, you will make $1000, but you then have to pay expenses such as cleaning staff, electric, water, etc. to cover the ten rooms.

Now raise your rates to $300 a night. If only half of the hotel is full, you're now making $1500, more than you were making with a full hotel before. Out of that $1500, you have to pay only half of the expenses you were paying.

Now apply these principles to any item or service you can imagine and when the customers complain about the high prices blame the cost of gasoline, the "shrinking dollar," the growth of the middle class in China and India, or any other topic popular in the news at that moment.

That's it. That's the whole trick. It's that simple. Once you understand that all of these prices are essentially imaginary, you can be empowered to go out and get the goods and services you need at the real prices, any way you can.

I don't care who you are, where you live, or what you buy. All of the protesting, petitioning, boycotting, lobbying and letter writing is never going to accomplish a thing. If you want to bring about real change, positive change, then look no further than your wallet, your credit cards, and how you intend to use them. Find any way to get the goods and services you need as cheaply (if not for free) as possible so long as it's legal and ethical. Take advantage of any promotion that pays you money to acquire a product (whether you need it or not), and donate the product to someone who could really use it if you do not have any interest in it. Corporate America won't know what to do with itself when it discovers a nation draining its resources by using the very marketing tools it depends on to sell unnecessary products.

That is true Retail Anarchy and I hope you will adopt it as your "lifestyle brand" (don't worry, this one doesn't cost anything and you won't have to wear any funny clothes).

Let me take it off the one and put it on the four for a minute. On a recent hot summer day I found myself in the parking lot of a supermarket packing the car full of orange juice and ground beef. My cellphone rang and it was Jean asking me to pick her up at the subway station. I finished loading up the car (as usual, to the point that it was impossible to see out of most of the windows) and drove over, listening to Shelia E's "Romance 1600" album.

As I pulled up to the subway stop, which is located next to the parking lot of another supermarket, I realized that the reason Jean wanted me to pick her up was that she had found a deal on who knows what, but was standing there with several shopping bags of her own which were too heavy to carry home. I parked the car but left the motor running to keep the air conditioner blasting on my now slow-cooking ground beef and lukewarm orange juice. I just love turning a Toyota Corolla into a $20,000 crockpot.

Anyway, there we are, standing on the sidewalk, trying to figure out how we are going to get all of this crap in the car in a timely manner, when the whole conversation turns into the two of us having battling temper tantrums. "Dear Michaelangelo" has long since ended, and we stop screaming at each other long enough to look up and realize that three quarters of the parking lot is now dancing to "A Love Bizarre" which is pouring out of our car's windows. "We got them moving," I said, "now we just have to get them to think." With that, I smiled and said, "Wanna dance?" Jean smacked me in the head, then took my hand and we danced around a car full of rotting meat. (You can throw up now.)

DATE DUE

BRODART, CO.

Cat. No. 23-221